A MICROSIMULATED TRANSACTIONS MODEL OF THE UNITED STATES ECONOMY

A Microsimulated Transactions Model of the United States Economy

Robert L. Bennett and Barbara R. Bergmann

THE JOHNS HOPKINS UNIVERSITY PRESS
Baltimore and London

The Johns Hopkins University Press, 701 West 40th Street
Baltimore, Maryland 21211
The Johns Hopkins Press Ltd., London

The paper in this book is acid-free and meets the guidelines for
permanence and durability of the Committee on Production Guidelines
for Book Longevity of the Council on Library Resources.

Library of Congress Cataloging-in-Publication Data

Bennett, Robert L., 1931–
    A microsimulated transactions model of the United States economy.

    Bibliography: p.
    Includes index.
    1. United States—Economic conditions—1981-   —Econometric models. 2. United
States—Economic conditions—1981-   —Data processing.   I. Bergmann, Barbara
R. II. Title.
HC106.8.B46   1985   330.973'00724   85-45049
ISBN 0-8018-2878-3 (alk. paper)

Contents

viii   Contents

Figures

Tables

Acknowledgments

The authors would like to acknowledge the expert and assiduous research assistance of William T. Sutton during three of the twelve years this project has taken. We were the beneficiaries of National Science Foundation grant APR77-14693. Finally, the project would not have been possible without massive gifts of computer time from the University of Maryland Computer Science Center.

A MICROSIMULATED TRANSACTIONS MODEL
OF THE UNITED STATES ECONOMY

Chapter 1. Introduction

All analyses by economists of the determinants of macroeconomic magnitudes—aggregate output, average price levels, unemployment rates—have to some extent been based on purported descriptions of the behavior of individual decisionmakers and descriptions of their interactions. Formally speaking, however, the conventional macroeconomic models we have known, from the early work of Klein and Goldberger down to the present models of Klein, Eckstein, Evans, Almon, and others, consist of collections of macroeconomic equations; in each such equation, one macroeconomic magnitude is dependent on other macroeconomic magnitudes (Klein and Goldberger 1955; Duesenberry et al. 1965; Evans 1969; Almon 1965). Descriptions of individual behavior do figure in the making of those models—they influence which macroequations are chosen and the variables that appear in each. However, there is little or no place in the traditional macroequations for the formal incorporation of any qualitative description of individual or institutional behavior.

The research effort laid out in this book represents an attempt to move away from macroeconomics through macroequations; it attempts to integrate the description of individuals' and firms' behavior more closely into the formal structure of a model that is macroeconomic mainly in the sense that its purpose is the determination of aggregates. The model we present here is microsimulated—it consists entirely of explicit descriptions of decisionmaking and the consequent actions and interactions of individual decisionmakers. The model's action on the macroeconomic level is made completely consistent with the action on the microeconomic level, since the macro derives exactly from the micro. This is accomplished by adding the microeconomic results into the macroeconomic results numerically, by computer.

The introduction into economics of the basic idea on which our model is based is due to Guy Orcutt (1960, 1976). He and economists working with him have pioneered the construction of models of the household sector in which groups of representative individuals and families are delineated as following certain postulated behavior rules. Models of the type introduced by Orcutt have been used extensively by the federal government of the United States to characterize the first-round results of government policies having direct impact on the household sector. They have been particularly useful in gauging the distributional effects of such policies, as well as their effects on aggregates such as total labor force and population size. A methodologically similar research effort is the analysis of the structure of the personal income tax by Joseph Pechman and Benjamin Okner (1974). Their work depicts individual families paying taxes according to historic or hypothetical versions of the federal income-tax code and has been used to study the effects of tax-code changes on total revenues and on the distribution of tax liabilities among taxpayers.

Other pioneers of microsimulation methodology include Frederic L. Pryor (1973) and Alan S. Blinder (1974), who utilized it to study the mechanics of income distribution. Ray Fair (1974) has the distinction of being the first to apply such methods to macroeconomic issues. Irma Adelman and Sherman Robinson (1978) microsimulated production, price formation, and income distribution in a developing economy. Donald A. Nichols (1980) has used microsimulation to study the unemployment/inflation nexus. The behavior of firms with respect to competition and innovation and the consequences of that behavior for long-run growth have been studied with microsimulation methods by Richard R. Nelson, Sydney G. Winter, and Herbert L. Schuette (1976) and Richard R. Nelson and Sydney G. Winter (1982).

Our microsimulation work is closest in form to that of groups led by Orcutt and that of Pechman and Okner. However, their work has been restricted to one major sector of the economy—the household sector. Our work (and the contemporaneous work of Gunnar Eliasson [1976] in Sweden) also microsimulates the household sector but extends the methodology to the business and government sectors. This results in a model that can be used to study the effects of policies whose primary impact is on business firms. It can also be used to investigate the full effects (as opposed to just the primary impact) of any policy, as those effects are passed back and forth from sector to sector. The unique advantage of the microsimulation methodology—the ability it gives the analyst to characterize government policies in a way that reflects their essential features—is thus extended and developed in our model, which we characterize as the Transactions Model, to highlight the level at which activities are represented. In this book, the aptness of the model for policy studies is displayed by applications to two subjects: the fiscal and monetary effects of the issuance of indexed bonds and the employment and productivity effects of changes in the scheduled hours of work.

Major Features of the Transactions Model

The behavior represented in the Transactions Model is the familiar repertoire on which macroeconomists have traditionally focused—consumption, saving, money holding, financial-asset acquisition, real investment, production, employment, wage setting, price setting, and interest-rate setting. This model differs from conventional models in the methodology of representing the behaviors. Major features of the model are:

1. The decisionmakers whose behavior is simulated in the model are ten firms who among them produce the economy's goods and nonfinancial services; a bank; a financial intermediary; a federal government; a state/local government; a monetary authority; and 700-plus employed and unemployed workers who are members of households that consume and that hold assets.

2. Each individual decisionmaker's experience and situation in the simulated economy are kept track of and enter into the decisionmaking process. On the occasion of any action on the microeconomic level (such as a transaction), the variables that record the situation of the individuals involved in it are changed appropriately. For example, making a purchase for cash results in a reduced money balance recorded in the computer for the purchaser, whereas taking a loan results in an increased money balance recorded for the borrower.

3. The interaction of individual decisionmakers takes the form of transactions between individual buyers and sellers, in which goods, services, or claims are exchanged against money. Thus, the monetary and real sides are integrated in the model's simulated economy precisely as they are in the actual economy. The events treated as transactions in the model, in addition to purchases of the output of the firms, include loans, amortization of loans, payment of taxes, payment of interest, payment of wages, and transfer payments.

4. Each time a transaction occurs, the effect of that transaction on all simulated macroeconomic variables—nominal GNP accounts, flow-of-funds accounts, price indexes, and so on—is recorded. Values of endogenous macrovariables are changed in no other way. All of the usual macroeconomic variables are thus simulated by the model on a basis consistent with the portrayed action on the microeconomic level. The use of an unchanging, multiplicative scale factor brings the macroeconomic output up to the scale of the U.S. economy.

5. The model operates on the assumption that all decisions controlling behavior are made once a week, on the basis of the position of the decisionmaker at the time of the decision. The model is thus completely recursive; there is no simultaneity. Although the microeconomic behavior underlying aggregate variables is taken to be adjusted weekly by the decisionmakers, each simulated aggregate is accumulated for the time interval for which the corresponding U.S. data series is available: monthly for employment and unemployment, and quarterly for the components of the national income accounts and the flow-of-funds accounts.

6. Economic data for the United States have been used to construct the data base for the model and to fit the parameters of behavioral rules specified for the actors in the model.

Ideally, the novel form of the Transactions Model should be matched with appropriate novelties in econometric methodology. We cannot pretend that we have, at this writing, advanced very far in the development of techniques for parameter estimation especially suitable to models of this type. We have used macroeconomic data almost exclusively. For some of the behavioral equations, we have adapted a simple version of the iterative-search techniques used to simulate engineering problems. For others, where it seemed to give a reasonable result, we have, with some reluctance, used the standard techniques for dealing with parameter estimation in conventional macroeconomic models—fitting macroequations and translating the result onto the microeconomic level.

Data Bases for the Transactions Model

Microsimulation models of the Orcutt or Pechman/Okner type use samples of actual households and apply the behavior patterns they postulate to the individuals in the sample. Such a sample serves as the data base of the simulation. The information about the characteristics of each individual contained in the data base is used to determine, in part, the nature of the simulated behavior and the nature of the simulated outcome for that individual. For example, in Orcutt's model, a person's age, marital status, sex, and number and ages of children affect that person's labor-force participation. In the Pechman/Okner model, a person's marital status affects the basis on which taxes are figured.

In the Transactions Model, the data base for households has been constructed out of microdata from the Bureau of Labor Statistics' Consumer Expenditure Survey (CES) of 1972–73. These data contain information about income from financial assets by type, and from them we have estimated a portfolio of assets for the year of the CES for each of the households into which the simulated individuals are collected. The CES also contains information about labor-force participation, marital status, car ownership, home ownership, and occupation.

An analogous procedure is, in principle at least, available for firms. Information on the income accounts and balance sheets of large and medium-sized firms is publicly available in the United States, and a sample of actual firms might thus have been used as a data base for the business sector. In constructing the business sector of the Transactions Model, however, it became apparent that constraints on computer time and real time made it desirable to keep the number of firms, in this initial version at least, quite small. We needed to retain a large number of items of information about the current and past position of each firm, many more than were retained for each labor-force member. This reflects the fact that the repertoire of behavior of the firm is considerably more extensive and complex than that of the individual. (Over 300 words of information are stored concerning each firm, and only twenty seven-words for each labor-force member.) In the version of the model presented here, we have represented only twelve firms. Obviously, no set of twelve U.S. firms drawn randomly or selected in any other way could be representative of the business sector of the U.S. economy.

A second consideration, which would have operated even had the number of simulated firms been considerably larger, was the desirability of representing the flows of particular product groups between firms, from firms to households, and from firms to governments. We wanted to distinguish flows of vehicles, other manufactured durables, manufactured nondurables, agriculture, mineral extraction, banking services, capital-intensive services, and other services. This consideration suggested that the most appropriate decisionmaking unit for the business sector of the Transactions Model is the business establishment (a production site devoted to a particular type of product) rather than a business firm (not infrequently a conglomerate of establishments producing a wide variety of products). Nevertheless, we use the term *firm* to indicate these businesses.

Each firm in the Transactions Model is constructed with characteristics representative of a particular industry group in its input/output relations, age distribution, size and characteristics of its capital stock, debt and asset structure, cost structure, and profit margin. We set the characteristics of these representative firms by using data in the national income and product accounts and flow-of-funds accounts of the United States. For example, for the firm representative of nondurable manufacturing, the time series of investment in capital equipment by nondurable manufacturing establishments was used to construct the characteristics and age distribution of the stock of producing equipment.

In one important respect, the Transactions Model's firms are not at all representative of actual establishments. The size of each simulated firm (the value of its output, size of its labor force, and so on) is governed by the aggregate size of the corresponding U.S. industry, rather than by the size of individual establishments in that industry. Thus an industry consisting of relatively small establishments (the "other services" industry, for example, which includes law firms; or the "trade" industry, which includes retail stores) is represented in the model by a firm that may be as large as the firm representing automobile manufacturing.

The one-firm-per-industry method of representing the business sector obviously poses limitations on the kinds of problems that can be studied with the Transactions Model in the form we present it here. Applications in which competition among firms in an industry and the distribution of an industry's business activity among its firms are of crucial concern could not be fruitfully made. Nevertheless, the treatment of the firm in the Transactions Model, despite the synthetic construction of the business-sector data base, does offer certain considerable advantages over conventional macroeconomic models, even over those that give detailed treatment to input/output relationships among industries. Among other things, each firm in the model has the ability to remember its debts and pay interest on them, to reflect the acquisition of cost-saving equipment in its pricing decision, and to examine the age distribution and productivity of its currently owned capital equipment when making investment decisions. Representation of such processes gives us the possibility of studying in a realistic framework a wide variety of government policies that impinge on firms' decisionmaking, operations, and environment.

Decisionmaking and Its Consequences in the Transactions Model

Most economists who specialize in microeconomics construct theories of behavior that have as their mainspring the attempt at maximization of some quantity—utility in the case of the consumer, profit in the case of the business firm. Many macroeconomists have been rather looser in their descriptions of individual behavior, tending simply to postulate the direction of individuals' reactions to changes in their economic environment, frequently without recourse to rigorous maximization modeling. A microsimulated model, such as the one presented here, would seem to be an ideal vehicle for the incorporation of the virtues of microeconomic theory into macroeconomics. This is the tack taken in the simulation work of Ray Fair, who has created a model representing one firm and one consumer/worker, in which both actors decide on their upcoming behavior by solving optimal-control problems.

Unlike Fair, we have not embedded maximization submodels into the structure of the Transactions Model. In general, our actors use rather simple rules of thumb in deciding what to do, although of course these rules take account of conditions the actors face in ways that previously developed maximization models might certainly suggest. While we would not wish to argue that a macroeconomic model based on microtheoretic methods is not a worthwhile objective, our efforts have been directed toward different goals.

One of our aims has been the development of a more exact and faithful accounting and depiction of what might be characterized as the semi-automatic consequences of behavioral decisions. To take an example, a decision to borrow and a decision to lend result in a loan, and from these decisions a considerable number of consequences come about. The loan takes the form of a flow of funds from the lender to the borrower. Later flows of funds to take care of interest and amortization occur; the rated capacity of the borrower for future borrowings and the capacity of the lender to make further loans change; the flow of goods and services financed by the proceeds of the loan occurs; the future income of the lender is affected. None of these consequences requires any decisionmaking complex enough to attract the interest of economic theorists, yet they are all of considerable practical importance. In the Transactions Model, we handily represent all of these consequences as occurring, and the effects of these consequences on future decisions and future behavior can be allowed for.

Over 90 percent of the computer code in which the Transactions Model is written depicts interactions between decisionmakers that follow on decisions. One commentator on our work has characterized this elaboration of the consequences of decisionmaking as an emphasis on accounting, albeit in a rather expanded sense of that word. A somewhat more sympathetic way of putting the same idea is that we have paid a great deal of detailed attention to the kinds of behavioral activity that in most macroeconomic models are taken care of in a cursory way under the heading of accounting identities—or are not taken care of at all. We have elaborated our treatment of the consequences of decisionmaking in the belief that a careful accounting for and depiction of these kinds of behavioral activity brings important advantages. Such an accounting improves the clarity of our understanding of economic processes and illuminates the process whereby the effects of exogenous shocks and policy changes are transmitted from one sector of the economy to the others.

A second goal to which we have directed our efforts in designing the Transactions Model is to provide a framework within which policies can be represented with a degree of realism greater than is possible in conventional macroeconomic models. The characterization in microsimulation models of the actors as individuals, each with a recorded history, represents a considerable increase in our ability to make realistic representations of policies, as experience with models of the Orcutt and Pechman/Okner variety has shown. For example, in the Transactions Model we have the capability to represent an excess-profits tax, with the definition of excess based on price changes, cost changes, profit changes, or any combination thereof. Or we can represent a subsidy program under which firms are rewarded for hiring workers who have had a spell of more than, say, twelve weeks of unemployment, because the computer can maintain a memory of how long each unemployed person has been unemployed. It can also remember how long each employed person has been with his or her present employer, so that a time limit on benefits to the employee can be incorporated if desired. To take another example, a change in the model's tax code in the direction of allowing for more accelerated depreciation directly affects the cash flow of our firms. Furthermore, the prospect that investment in a piece of equipment carries with it a delay in taxes paid out of profit can easily be made to affect the simulated firm's decision as to whether to purchase that piece of equipment. All that is required is that a subroutine be created in which the firm figures the present value of the interest-free loan from the government and subtracts this from the cost of the equipment.

The policy studies with the Transactions Model, which appear in the last chapter, have been chosen not only for their intrinsic interest but also to display the model's special capabilities in representing policies and their implementation.

Simultaneity in the Actual Economy and the Simulated Economy

Analyses of the macroeconomy traditionally represent the economy by simultaneous equations. Originally, simultaneous-equations formulations were developed to describe static systems, where the only movement contemplated was a shift of unspecified rapidity from one more-or-less long-lasting equilibrium to another. The time periods involved were generally left vague.

When empirical macromodels based on time-series data began to be estimated, the simultaneous-equations formulation was carried over, but with the time dimension of the analysis more explicitly specified. The basic period of the analysis generally was taken to be identical with the shortest period for which all the data were available (the data period), and the system was solved anew for each data period. This use of the simultaneous-equations formulation can be thought of as an adaptation to the fact that available data on economic activity are averaged out or aggregated over time periods that are so long that the actors must react more than once in a data period to actions of others in the same period. Within a calendar quarter, for example, there is time for a fall in production, a resulting reduction in consumption, and the reaction to this of production. The simultaneous solution of behavioral equations that specify such reactions purports to represent the stable situation, after all of these actions and reactions have taken place and behavior has settled into a pattern in which all actions are mutually consistent (in the sense that no decisionmaker wishes to act differently, given everyone else's behavior). If we were to think concretely (perhaps, some might say, to the point of mistaken concreteness) of what kind of economic system might be exactly represented by an empirical, quarterly simultaneous-equations model, it would be an economy where law requires that a *tatonnement* take place before business hours on the first day of each quarter and that activity proceed at the steady pace thus determined for all the rest of the days of the quarter.

In the Transactions Model, the fact that within a data period there can be multiple interactions among the actors is dealt with in a different way, which we believe provides somewhat greater realism. We have done away with the identity of the data period and the basic period of analysis and have disaggregated the data period into shorter periods, taking as the basic period of analysis a time interval so short that is is plausible to represent each actor as revising each type of decision only once during it. We represent each calendar quarter as being made up of twelve such basic periods; the basic period thus corresponds approximately to a week of real time. Within each basic period, a complete round of economic events is scheduled.

The construction of an entirely recursive model (with respect to the basic operating periods rather than the data periods) does more than advance somewhat the cause of realism. It also saves us from the surely tedious and perhaps infeasible chore of simultaneously solving all the behavioral equations. Put another way, the elimination of simultaneity (in the sense of multiple intraperiod reactions) frees us to postulate realistic behavior rules (if we know any) without having to worry that the mathematics of the solution process will be too difficult. As noted above, in the present version of the model, we have not used this freedom to go beyond our macroeconomist precedessors in the elaboration of the decisionmaking process but only in the elaboration of the practical consequences of the decisions.

The one form of simultaneity actually observed in economic life is, of course, the coincidence in time of economic events—many acts of production, consumption, and exchange go on at the same time, and some go on continuously. In depicting the actions of individual actors on the computer, one is constrained to represent all actions by computations that are bound to occur sequentially. Regarded retrospectively, it does not matter whether two economic events are represented as occurring simultaneously or in immediate sequence if the occurrence of one event does not affect the likelihood, feasibility, or characteristics of the other. The adoption of a short basic period reduces the implausibility of removing all coincidence in time and the implausibility of representing activities that are continuous in the real world by action concentrated at particular instants.

In the operation of the Transactions Model, the ability of an actor to carry out a decision is usually not affected by whether that actor is first or last in line to implement the decision, since in the real world and in the simulated world that mimics it, there is usually ample excess capacity. In the rare case of temporary shortages, however, the ability of individuals to carry out decisions is affected by whether they are early or late within a round to try to engage in a transaction. In such a case, the model prescribes procedures for the rationing of goods in short supply, so that latecomers are not closed out in favor of complete fulfillment of orders by earlier customers. This occurs most importantly in the allocation of labor among firms when the unemployment rate is very low.

Treatment of Expectations

A simulation model provides an excellent opportunity for the incorporation of material on expectations. In the context of such a model, it is relatively easy to represent individual actors as forming expectations concerning future economic environments by any method thought to be a realistic representation of how decisionmakers actually do form them—by taking moving averages, by using Box/Jenkins (1976) extrapolation methods, or even by formulating, fitting, and forecasting with a conventional macromodel of considerable complexity. The simulation model can also show how the actors react to the expectations they form—it can present an elaboration of how expectations affect the actors' decisions.

The reader may well judge that in building the present version of the Transactions Model we have taken rather scant advantage of these opportunities for dealing with expectations. Expectations of the future are shown in the model as entering only into those of our actors' decisions from which considerable damage is possible if the future is very different from the present.[1] Most decisions in the model, such as those having to do with what price to charge, how much to produce, or which job to accept, are relatively easily compensated for in the short run and thus can be made on the assumption that things will remain much as they are at the moment of decision. If this expectation proves false, new decisions, which repair the situation without much damage, can usually be made and implemented.

We have represented the formation and use of expectations by the actors in two areas of decisionmaking: one is the investment by firms in new capital equipment, and the other is the adjustment by firms and households of their portfolios of financial assets. In the case of real investment, firms make simple forecasts of their near-term future output. They then use these forecasts to decide whether to produce the forecasted output on their currently owned equipment or to produce some of it on newly acquired equipment. Output forecasts are made in the present version by a moving-average method. In the case of portfolio adjustment, the actors are made to favor long-term bonds over shorter-term bonds to a greater extent when they forecast that future long-term interest rates will be lower than they currently are. They make such forecasts when current long-term rates are higher than a moving average of past rates.

At this point, it is worth emphasizing that any piece of decisionmaking machinery currently in the model can easily be entirely replaced by another piece of machinery that makes the decision in question in a qualitatively different way. The ease of doing this is derived from the recursive structure of the model, which eliminates solution processes. Since individual components of the model may be replaced with great ease by very different ones, the present version of the model should be seen as a collection of hypothesized decision rules—many of which are by no means novel—assembled by means of a framework for which we claim considerable novelty. This framework would serve equally well for the assembly of a set of decision rules with different elements, elements perhaps more to the taste of the reader than those the authors have included in the present version. It is for the framework itself, rather than the details of any particular items of hypothesized behavior, that we claim the reader's attention and interest.

Chapter 2. Framework of the Transactions Model

In this chapter, we give summary descriptions of the actors represented in the Transactions Model, the commodities they produce and trade, and the financial assets they hold and exchange. We also give a brief account of the repertoire of behavior they are programmed to follow.

The Scale

The Transactions Model represents the U.S. economy by a simulated economy—one that is, of course, much smaller in scale than the actual. In any run of the model, whatever the historic calendar date taken to be the start of that run, the model's labor force starts out at 675 persons. A scale factor is used in each run to convert the output of the model's labor force (in conjunction of course, with the model's capital stock) into an output on the scale of that produced by the U.S. labor force:

$$\text{SCALE} = \frac{\text{historic size of U.S. labor force at starting period of run}}{675}$$

For example, for a run of the model with a starting period of January 1973, when the U.S. economy had 88.1 million persons in its labor force, the scale factor would be 130,519:1. The scale factor set at the beginning of a run holds throughout the run for physical production, physical capital, and financial stocks and flows, as well as for employment, unemployment, and labor force. In the course of a run, the size of the labor force and the pace of activity change as it tracks the historic course of the actual economy, but the scale does not change. It is as though we were studying actual railways by operating model railways and used HO scale for some runs and X scale for

Table 2.1. Characteristics of labor force, by occupational group (end of 1979)

Characteristic	Managers and Professionals	Clerks and Salespersons	Craft Workers and Operatives	Service Workers and Laborers[a]
Number employed	179	168	188	140
Number unemployed	3	7	12	10
Average weekly wage of employed (dollars)	391	240	324	175
Average value of assets (dollars)[b]	48,158	20,622	15,740	28,020
Proportion female	.27	.61	.20	.45
Proportion married	.67	.71	.59	.59
Proportion homeowners[b]	.63	.64	.67	.61

[a]Includes farm owners and operators.
[b]For married persons in different occupations, half of assets and homeownership is allocated to each occupational group.

other runs, adding or subtracting boxcars and tracks of the appropriate scale in the course of a run to represent growth and shrinkage of the system.

The Individuals

An individual in the simulated economy takes the form of an identification number and a vector of numbers in the computer memory, which represents information about his or her characteristics and economic situation. Labor-force members belong to one of four broad occupational groups, whose size and average attributes are shown in table 2.1. Persons not in the U.S. labor force who are in households that do include labor-force members are not directly represented in the model; consumer expenditures are made and assets are held by the household's labor-force members on their behalf. People not in the labor force who have financial assets are represented as individuals.[1] Households with no labor-force members and without financial assets are represented only as a group and receive transfer payments, which they use exclusively for purchasing consumer goods and services.

Labor-force members are differentiated by sex and marital status. An individual may be marked as the spouse of another individual in the labor force; their incomes and assets are treated as pooled, and their savings, consumptions, and asset management are determined jointly. Home ownership and car ownership are kept track of. On average, in the simulated economy as in the real one, members of the better-paid occupational groups have lower probability of unemployment, pay a higher average rate of personal taxes, have more assets, and obtain more income from assets. (In the current version of the model, age, educational attainment, and the number of household members apart from spouses are not explicitly represented.)

The number of persons represented as entering the labor force is influenced by the unemployment rate. The unemployed search for jobs by being available for random selection as a candidate when an employing firm seeks a worker in a particular occupational group. Their acceptance of a job may be affected by their eligibility for unemployment-insurance payments. A worker newly entering the labor force may apply for a job in any occupational group, subject to quotas that differ by sex. He or she ordinarily retains the occupational identity of the first job. A worker experienced in one occupation is allowed to become a candidate for an opening in another occupation only in times of shortages in the latter occupation.

After receiving their incomes, negotiating consumption loans, paying their taxes, and making payments on previous loans, households follow a Stone/Geary linear-expenditure system. Although all are assumed to have the same tastes, they spend differing amounts because of their differing assets, differing incomes, and differing past expenditures. In their portfolio management, they compare rates of return of the various available assets and vary the mix of assets they hold according to relative rates of return. The size of the portfolio each household has to manage at any point in a run of the model depends on the assets assigned to it at the beginning of the run and on the sum of previous savings decisions.

The Firms

Private production of goods and nonfinancial services in the simulated economy is divided into ten firms, each of which represents a U.S. industry group. In addition, there are a bank and a financial intermediary which are set up as service-producing firms but which also maintain the actors' financial accounts and set interest rates. Table 2.2 lists these firms and their contributions to various aggregates.

For each run of the model, a physical unit of output of each firm is defined as the amount of its product that could have been bought in the starting period with one dollar. Physical units of capital goods, called machines, are also defined for each run of the model on a physical basis. A machine is specialized to the firm in which it is used and is defined as a bundle of the outputs of up to eight of the twelve firms (see table 2.2). The machine bundle is scaled in physical units so as to cost one dollar in the starting period. The physical quantities of the goods that make up a machine

Table 2.2. Firms and their employment and output (starting January 1980)

ID Number	Firm	Employment White Collar	Blue Collar	Share of Output Value	Share of Machine for Firm 5
1	Agriculture	0	19	0.057	0.000
2	Mining	1	4	0.037	0.000
3	Construction	7	28	0.063	0.244
4	Automobile manufacturing	1	3	0.029	0.086
5	Other durable manufacturing	24	52	0.177	0.600
6	Nondurable manufacturing	16	35	0.184	0.000
7	Capital-intensive services	9	23	0.096	0.006
8	Trade	85	56	0.113	0.062
9	Other services	86	50	0.162	0.002
10	Real estate	6	0	0.046	0.000
11	Financial intermediary	16	1	0.028	0.000
12	Bank	8	0	0.008	0.000

NOTE: Agriculture represents farming, forestry, and fisheries; mining represents all extractive industries; capital-intensive services represent transportation, communications, electric, gas, and sanitary services; real estate includes sales and rentals of dwelling units.

used by a particular firm are assumed not to change through time, although the cost of buying a new machine changes as output prices charged by the firms producing parts of the machine bundle change. The capital-goods setup of the model may be characterized as "clay-clay" (see Wonnacott [1978, 456–57]). A firm cannot choose among varieties of capital goods; it must buy the capital goods (appropriate for its type of output) currently on sale. Each machine is assumed to be born with a particular labor requirement and a particular rated output. A machine lasts fifteen years, and its operating characteristics improve over its lifetime, as a result of "disembodied" technical change—more educated workers and improved workplace organization.

A firm's capital goods are differentiated by quarterly acquisition date; the more recently produced physical units of capital goods are assumed to have better output/labor ratios than units from older vintages. Typically, a new machine gives more output in a standard workweek and requires fewer workers for the production of its rated output than machines produced in the preceeding period. The rates of change of the output capabilities and labor-input requirements of newly produced machines of successive vintages are among the basic parameters of the model, since they are an important component of productivity change.

Purchases by each firm of the outputs of others as noncapital inputs to current production (flow inputs) are governed by the 1972 input/output table, and are taken to be unchanging over the time period of the simulation and to be unaffected by capital-goods purchases.

Firms have U-shaped, short-run average cost curves for two familiar reasons: the presence of substantial fixed costs and a rising marginal cost. Larger outputs cause the firm to bring into production successively older vintages of capital goods with smaller output/labor ratios. A firm's cost curve shifts whenever the prices of labor and flow inputs change; it also shifts when investment results in the acquisition of new capital goods, which are more labor saving than the best of the old capital stock.

Firms set prices in the course of each round on a cost-plus basis, and sell to all customers at that price. They set output for each round so as to allow inventory to approach a desired ratio to a moving average of sales. They set desired employment by a lagged adjustment to production, making adjustments in weekly hours to achieve man-hour targets for the current week. Their portfolio management and borrowing activities depend on their cash inflow from sales, cash outflow for purchases and dividend payments, and investment plans. Like consumers, they are sensitive to current and expected relative rates of return when choosing the form in which to hold their financial assets. In making decisions about investment in capital goods, firms forecast future sales and consider the costs of operation of their older equipment, the purchase price and operation cost of newly available equipment, and the cost of the funds to finance the purchase.

The Financial Institutions

Two of the firms, the bank and the financial intermediary, have the special function of providing financial services to the other actors. At the end of each round they set the interest rates that will apply to newly issued debt in the subsequent round.

The bank gives bank loans on request to all of the nongovernment actors, up to a limit on outstanding stock of loans for each actor. All of the cash held by the actors is a liability of the bank (as are all the savings deposits), and cash is created by payments from the bank to other actors and is destroyed by the reverse. The bank must observe reserve requirements, and it changes interest rates on new bank loans in accordance with its reserve position. Among its assets, the bank holds mortgages, government bills and bonds, and loan instruments.

The financial intermediary makes a market in open-market securities (such as treasury bills, treasury bonds, and private securities) by buying all that it is offered and making all requested sales. It raises interest rates on newly issued securities when the supply exceeds demand enough that the size of its holdings increases above that which it wishes to hold; it lowers interest rates in the opposite case. It adjusts prices of previously issued securities to accord with the current interest rates.

The Governmental Entities

Three actors in the model represent the government sector: a federal government, a state/local government, and a monetary authority.

The federal government collects personal income taxes each round from the households by setting rules for exempted income and applying a schedule of marginal rates to nonexempted income. It also collects excise, corporate-profits, and payroll taxes. It employs some of the labor force, makes purchases from the firms, and makes unemployment-insurance payments and other transfer payments. When it runs a deficit, it issues new bonds and bills, which are sold for cash to the financial intermediary, through which they are sold to the other actors. Bills and bonds coming due are paid off or rolled over. The operation of the state/local government is similar to that of the federal government, with some differences in function and in scale.

The monetary authority conducts open-market operations by transactions with the financial intermediary. It sets a reserve ratio and a maximum interest rate for savings accounts. It also influences the amount of the bank's discounting by setting a discount rate.

The Rest-of-World

The rest-of-world sector is depicted in the model as a firm that purchases exports from U.S. firms and sells imports to U.S. firms and households. It holds a portfolio of claims on the U.S. firms and governments and issues liabilities and equities held by U.S. firms and households. This sector does not directly employ any labor. It sells to the other actors from an unconstrained inventory of specific commodities and financial assets at prices and quantities set exogenously. Its purchases from U.S. firms are at exogenously determined quantities but endogenously determined prices.

In addition to these transactions in goods and services, the rest-of-world receives transfers from the federal government in the amount indicated in the national accounts. It makes payments to the bank and the financial intermediary for interest on its debt obligations and receives interest on its portfolio, in amounts consistent with the net values of interest and dividends from the national accounts. The rest-of-world also receives payment from and makes payment to the monetary authority for the authority's purchases or sales of foreign exchange, which are set at the level indicated in the flow-of-funds accounts. Holdings of financial assets and issues of financial liabilities by the rest-of-world are forced to conform with the flow-of-funds accounts.

Running the Model

Each run of the model is done for a particular reason or set of reasons: projecting into the future or rerunning the past with policies or conditions different from those actually in force. The purpose of each run, of course, governs the detailed form of the run, but the general outline is similar for all runs.

A run of a conventional macroeconomic model requires that values for macroeconomic variables appearing in lagged form in any of the model's equations be supplied as initial conditions. Setting up the initial conditions for a run of the Transactions Model is a considerably more demanding task, requiring that each actor be assigned values for those variables that will underlie his or her first round of decisions. At the start of each run, firms are supplied with (1) initial values of capital stock, distributed by vintage, (2) inventories of stocks of their own and other firms' goods, (3) initial prices, and (4) financial assets and liabilities of various types and maturities. Workers are supplied with (1) the identity of their employer, if employed, (2) the length of their spell of unemployment, if unemployed, (3) assets, (4) liabilities, (5) recent level of expenditures, (6) sex, (7) martial status, and (8) the identity of the spouse if married.

As in a macromodel, the initial conditions for a run of the Transactions Model depend on the historic period chosen for the starting period. An account of the methodology of creating initial conditions is given in the next chapter, where the use of data both for setting initial conditions and for parameter estimation is considered in detail.

Once the initial microconditions have been set up, the actors are programmed to go through their behavioral routines in a fixed sequence. Twelve times each calendar quarter, a round of microeconomic events occurs—the actors go through the entire repertoire of decisions or activities in the regularly scheduled order of table 2.3 (the chapter in which it is detailed follows each event).

A decision at one step influences events later in the round; for example, wage-setting decisions influence household expenditures for goods and services, which in turn influence the demand for financial assets.

The round starts with a decision by each firm on how much of its product it prefers to produce. The decision is based on its inventory position and on sales in the recent past. The firm then decides how many people it wants to lay off or hire and tries to carry out these decisions by interviewing unemployed workers. The number of workers aboard and the distribution of

Table 2.3. Sequence of events in a round

Event	Chapters In Which Event Is Described In Detail
1. Firms make tenative production decisions.	4
2. Firms make decisions on hiring and weekly hours.	4
3. Workers are laid off or quit; firms and governments search for workers to hire; workers search for jobs; workers are hired.	4
4. Firms set wage rates for each occupation.	4
5. Production occurs, affecting firms' inventories.	4
6. Firms compute cost, profits, and taxes owed.	4
7. Each firm sets price for its product.	4
8. Firms purchase flow inputs from other firms.	4
9. Firms pay taxes to governments.	4,5
10. Firms make investment decisions and purchase capital goods.	4
11. Real-estate firm makes decision concerning housing stock.	4
12. Events which give rise to inputed items in GNP but no flow of funds.	5,6
13. Firms and governments pay wages	5
14. Government makes transfer payments to unemployed.	5,7
15. Some households receive property income.	5
16. Households pay income and social security taxes to government.	5,7
17. Households make payments on mortgages and bank loans.	5,6
18. Households make decisions about home and car ownership.	5
19. Households make consumption decisions and purchase goods and services.	5
20. Households make portfolio-management decisions and take action on them.	5
21. Government purchases goods and services from firms.	7
22. Rest-of-world sells to and purchases from firms.	4
23. Government makes debt-management decisions and takes action.	6,7
24. Nonfinancial firms make finance and liquidity decisions and take consequent actions.	4
25. Financial intermediary adjusts cash position.	6
26. Monetary authority makes decisions and takes action on open market.	7
27. Bank reacts to reserve position: sets loan policy; discounts with monetary authority; sells or buys open-market securities.	6
28. Financial intermediary readjusts cash position.	6
29. Bank sets current interest rates for consumer loans, business loans, mortgages, and savings accounts.	6
30. Financial intermediary sets current bill and bond rate.	6
31. Government and nonfinancial firms pay interest on existing obligations at original rate to financial intermediary; firms pay dividends.	4,5
32. Financial intermediary pays interest to nonfinancial firms on their holdings of bonds and bills.	6

the firm's capital stock by vintage determine the amount produced. At this point, production occurs in the form of a drawdown of the firm's inventories of material inputs and an increase in its inventory of its own output. Wage and price decisions by the firm follow, and it replenishes its materials inventories by purchases from other firms. The firm pays taxes, makes investment decisions, and receives lagged shipments of previously ordered capital goods from those firms whose products constitute parts of the machine bundle.

In the next sequence of events, household members receive wages and property and transfer income, pay taxes, and make interest and amortization payments on their outstanding debts. They then make their decisions on consumption, in the course of which they may increase or decrease their outstanding debt. At this point, they adjust the composition of their assets portfolios, transferring funds between cash and savings accounts and buying or selling securities.

Next, the federal and state/local governments purchase goods and services from the firms. (Government payments of wages to its own employees occurred in step 13, while interest payments by governments on their outstanding debts occur in step 31.)

The rest of the activity in the round is taken up by an assortment of financial dealings and decisions. The governments issue bills and bonds to take care of deficits and rollovers and allocate their financial assets among cash and open-market securities. The monetary authority makes its open-market purchases or sales of foreign exchange and domestic securities to bring actual bank reserves to the desired level, in accordance with open-market policy. It sets the discount rate, the maximum savings-account rate, and the reserve ratio. Next, the commercial bank calculates its excess or deficient reserves and makes its decisions to discount and to increase or decrease its holdings of open-market securities. It has made loans at interest rates announced at the end of the last round, and its loan inventory may have undergone (within limits) involuntary changes that reflect excess loan demand at current rates. On the basis of the sign and magnitude of the excess demands for bank loans, the bank adjusts the savings-account rate, the business-loan rate, and the consumer-loan rate.

At this point in the round, all portfolios have been adjusted, with the exception of the portfolio of the financial intermediary. The latter makes the market in open-market securities, having purchased or sold all that were offered or demanded at yields announced at the beginning of the round. On the basis of excess demand or supply for open-market securities, it adjusts rates for treasury bills, treasury bonds, state and local bonds, private bonds, and home mortgages.

The round ends with interest and dividend payments by governments and firms. They are sent in bulk to the bank that distributes these funds to households in the subsequent round.

Table 2.4. Market participation by sector

Sector	Input Markets		Final-Demand Markets				Financial Markets — Long-Term Claims					Financial Markets — Short-Term Claims					
	Labor Services	Interfirm Purchases	Consumer Goods	Fixed Capital	Net Exports	Government Purchases	Corporate Bonds	Federal Bonds	State/Local Bonds	Mortgages	Equities	Treasury Bills	Bank Loans	Money	Time & Savings Deposits	Discounts & Advances	Bank Reserves
Households																	
Labor-force households	S		D			S	D	D	D	S	D	D	D	D	D		
Other households			D											D	D		
Nonfinancial firms																	
Agriculture	D	DS	S	DS	DS	S	DS	D	D		S	D	D	D			
Mining	D	DS	S	D	DS	S	DS	D	D		S	D	D	D			
Construction	D	DS	S	DS	DS	S	DS	D	D		S	D	D	D			
Automobile manufacturing	D	DS	S	DS	DS	S	DS	D	D		S	D	D	D			
Other durable manufacturing	D	DS	S	DS	DS	S	DS	D	D		S	D	D	D			
Nondurable manufacturing	D	DS	S	D	DS	S	DS	D	D		S	D	D	D			
Capital-intensive service	D	DS	S	DS	DS	S	DS	D	D		S	D	D	D			
Trade	D	DS	S	DS	DS	S	DS	D	D		S	D	D	D			
Other service	D	DS	S	DS	DS	S	DS	D	D		S	D	D	D			
Real estate	D	DS	S	DS	DS	S	DS	D	D	S	S	D	D	D			
Financial firms																	
Financial intermediary	D	DS	S	DS	DS	S	DS	D	D	D	S	D	D	D	S		
Bank	D	DS	S	D	DS	S	DS	D	D	D	S	D	S	S	S	S	D
Government[a]																	
Federal	D	DS	S			DS	D	S		D		S					
State/local	D	DS	S			DS	D	D	S			D		D			
Monetary authority							D	D				D				D	S
Rest-of-world	D	DS	S		DS	S	DS	D	D		DS	D	DS	DS			

NOTE: S and D indicate participation on the supply and demand side, respectively. In financial markets, those on the demand side may sell already existing claims in their possession, but only those on the supply side may create new ones.
aIncludes government enterprises.

21

Markets

Market participation by the actors is summarized in table 2.4, where each horizontal line represents participation of each actor as buyer or seller in each of the markets for a good or a financial claim. Prices in each of these markets are set once in a round by designated actors, and all transactions for an entire round proceed at that price. Inventories serve as buffer stocks, allowing for differences in supply and demand in the short run. The market-clearing equations of conventional macroeconomic models have been replaced by sets of behavioral specifications for those actors who set the prices and hold the buffer stocks of each commodity. They are required to decide on target levels for the stocks and to make adjustments in the price or the production of the item when disparities between amounts flowing out of the buffer stock and amounts flowing in drive the level of the stock away from the target. Inventories of goods and financial claims thus become central to the operation of the model's markets.

For goods and services produced by nonfinancial firms, prices are ordinarily set by producers on a cost-plus basis, and firms sell all they can at the set price. An exogenous shift upward in average costs is followed by a price adjustment, which leads in turn to a reduction in quantity demanded by households and by firms that use the product as a machine ingredient.[2] The extent of the reduction depends on what changes in other prices have been occurring. Changes in costs in the simulated economy also affect the demand for goods and services through their effects on incomes. If producers of goods and services are unable to replenish their buffer stocks to desired levels, either because they lack capital capacity or because supplies of labor or purchased inputs are insufficient, they are programmed to raise prices, even if profit margins are ample. Conversely, an undesired buildup of buffer stock is conducive to decisions to lower prices or delay price increases that might have occurred by reason of rising costs and narrowed profit margins.

Wage changes are made by firms and vary directly with productivity and cost-of-living change. The demand for labor is only in the medium run affected by wages. In the very shortest run, the demand for labor is based on the labor necessary to produce desired output using the existing stock of capital equipment, with desired output being based on sales and inventory levels. However, higher labor costs affect prices, which affect total demand and the distribution of demand among products. In the longer run, higher wages encourage the purchase of larger quantities of the new, more labor-saving capital equipment, which, when it is put in place, reduces the amount of labor required to meet a given production target.

The markets for financial claims are run along lines perhaps more congenial to neoclassical theorists. For each type of claim, the financial intermediary makes the market by buying and selling to all comers at a price set by itself. If it finds itself accumulating or decumulating inventory of an item beyond what it desires on its own account, it changes the price in the next round.

Transactions and the Flow of Funds

Every sale of goods and services engaged in by individuals in the simulated economy involves the passing of merchandise from one decisionmaker to another and the passing of demand deposits in the opposite direction. Each transaction is accomplished by a subroutine named TRANS, which is called into action whenever any decisionmaker buys anything from any other decisionmaker. TRANS is the principal means by which the interactions of decisionmakers are depicted, and it is also the principal means by which action on the microlevel is made to contribute to the GNP and the flow-of-funds accounting.

Before TRANS is brought into operation, the details of the transaction have already been decided upon: the identity of the buyer and seller, the identity of their cash accounts, the price, the number of physical units of the good to be traded, the inventory records of the seller, and the GNP account to which the transaction is to be credited, if any. The operation of a transaction is diagrammed in figure 2.1. Before the transaction is implemented, a check is made for the adequacy of the buyer's cash and the adequacy of the seller's inventory. If the transaction is feasible, the seller's inventory is drawn down and the buyer's inventory is increased by the number of units of the good traded. Money changes hands—the buyer's cash account diminishes and that of the seller increases. The appropriate GNP accounts are credited with the transaction if the transaction is on income and product account.

TRANS is used whenever money changes hands—for the purchase of commodities, labor, financial assets, as well as for the payment of taxes and the making of government transfer payments. It is the consistent use of this naturalistic mechanism that makes possible the automatic integration of real and nominal GNP accounts and the flow-of-funds accounts. TRANS also insures that all stocks (money, financial claims, and goods) are built up or drawn down in accordance with the flows that the microunits decide shall occur.

In some transactions, the merchandise being purchased may be merely a claim given up by the payee. For example, a tax payment purchases the cancellation of a claim for that amount by the government. A purchase results in a record of an inventory buildup of the merchandise by the purchaser only where such a record is useful in explaining the purchaser's subsequent conduct.

Table 2.5 summarizes all events in the model that trigger cash flows by

Table 2.5. Cash flows between sectors, by type

Sector Receiving Cash Flow	Sector Generating Cash Flow						
	Nonfinancial Firms	Households	Government	Financial Intermediary	Bank	Monetary Authority	Rest-of-World
Nonfinancial firms	IO purch. Invstmt. goods	Cons. goods & svcs. Cons. debt int./prin.[a]	Govt. goods & svcs.	IO purch. Invstmt. goods Home purch.[b] Home repair[b] Govt. sec. int./prin.[b] Bus. bonds[b]	IO purch. Invstmt. goods Loans		Exports
Households	Wages Cons. loans		Wages Transfer pmts.	Wages Cons. loans Home mortg. issues[b] Dividends[b] Govt. sec. int./prin.[b] Bond int./prin.[b]	Wages Cons. loans		
Government	IO purch. Sales taxes Profits taxes Payroll taxes	Cons. goods & svcs. Income taxes Soc. ins. taxes	IO purch. Federal grants in aid to state/local	IO purch. Sales taxes Profits taxes Payroll taxes Home taxes[b] Home mortg. int./prin.[b] Govt. sec. int./prin.[b]	IO purch. Sales taxes Profits taxes Payroll taxes	Note Tax	Exports

24

Financial intermediary	IO purch. Dividends[b] Bond int./prin.[b] Govt. sec. purch.[b] Bus. bond purch.[b]	Cons. svcs. Cons. debt int./prin. Home purch.[b] Home repair & taxes[b] Home mortg. int./prin.[b] Bond purch.[b]	Govt. goods & svcs. Govt. sec. int./prin.[b] Home mortg. purch.[b] Govt. sec. purch.[b]	IO purch.	IO purch. Dividends[b] Loans Home mortg. purch.[b] Govt. sec. purch. Bus. bond purch.	Govt. sec. purch.	Govt. sec. purch. Bus. sec. purch. Bond int./prin.
Bank	IO purch. Loan int./prin.	Cons. goods & svcs. Cons. debt int./prin. Deposits to svg. accts.	Govt. goods & svcs.	IO purch. Loan int./prin. Home mortg. int./prin.[b] Govt. sec. int./prin.[b] Bus. bond int./prin.[b]	IO purch.	Discounts	Exports Loan int./prin.
Monetary authority				Govt. bond int./prin.[b]			
Rest-of-world	IO purch.	Cons. goods & svcs.	IO purch. Transfers Govt. goods & svcs.	IO purchases Govt. sec. int./prin.[b] Bus. sec. int./prin.[b] Bonds[b]	IO purch. Loans	For. exch. purch.	

[a] int./prin. is interest and principal.
[b] Cash payments that accrue to financial intermediary in its capacity as agent for account of others or that are made by them in that capacity.

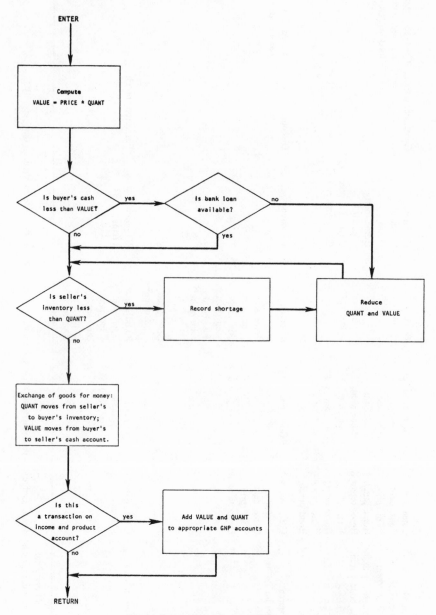

Figure 2.1. Diagram of a Transaction

source and destination of the flow. It includes flows on both current and capital account. Since every actor in the model has a cash account and each cash flow (with the exception of those in which the monetary authority is an actor) is accomplished by the building up of one cash account at the expense of another, the distribution of cash stocks at any moment in time is kept track of and may be printed out at will.

We have chosen to maintain the fiction that all of the open-market financial assets of households and firms are held for safekeeping by the financial intermediary, which collects the income due to owners of these assets and disburses it to the owners. This firm also buys and sells these assets for customers' accounts and makes the market in them. All payments are made by the transfer of demand deposits from one actor to another within the computer's memory. In this sense, the model mimics the world of the future, when all cash flows will be checkless and electronic.

Chapter 3. Fitting the Transactions Model with Data

The Transactions Model is an empirical model in the sense that we have assigned values to the parameters by employing algorithms that make use of data generated by the U.S. economy. Because of the special nature of the model, the methods developed for parameter estimation in conventional models could not have been used without considerable adaptation. This chapter discusses the problems inherent in estimating parameter values in microsimulation models, the alternatives in methodology, and the choices made in fitting the version of the model we present here. Later chapters present the estimates themselves, and display the ability of the model to track data beyond the period used to fit the parameters.

The Parameters

The Transactions Model is written in about ten-thousand lines of computer code. About 10 percent of the lines exist to tell the computer how to do the clerical work of keeping the records of the actors in usable and accurate form. The largest fraction of the code—almost 90 percent—is devoted to what we characterize in chapter 1 as the semiautomatic behavior that follows on decisionmaking. These lines activate such postdecision behavior as the transmission of cash to the seller and goods to the buyer's inventory after a purchase has been decided on, the amortization of and interest payment on previously decided upon loans, and the selling of bills by a government unit that has decided to run a deficit. Less than 1 percent of the code is devoted to the kinds of decisionmaking that economists have focused on—decisions on how much of each commodity to produce and how much of each commodity and each financial asset to sell or to buy at which price.

The model has 300 parameters. The vast majority of these parameters appear in the lines of computer code devoted to decisionmaking in the sense that is traditional among economists. Those few parameters that appear in the lines devoted to semiautomatic postdecision behavior are for the most part there to control the lags in delivery of items such as housing or fixed capital, which have considerable periods of production; parameters of this nature are fixed extraneously. The parts of the model devoted to semi-automatic postdecision behavior deal (although much more elaborately) with the same kinds of economic phenomena that are dealt with in a conventional model by accounting identities, which typically contain no parameters.

It is common practice in the economic literature to use the parameter-estimation process as a major ingredient in the validation of a model's structure. The lack of parameters in the postdecision behavior parts of the Transactions Model means that such parts—which constitute a major part of the model's apparatus—are excluded from whatever legitimacy is conferred by well-fitted regression equations. Accounting identities in conventional models are similarly excluded, but they tend to excite little controversy. Their validity seems obvious and goes unquestioned, and the importance of specifying them adequately has never been emphasized.

One purpose in elaborating the depiction of semiautomatic postdecision behavior is to improve the performance of the model when it is run to simulate periods outside the period of the data to which it is fitted. This elaboration should serve this end by improving the accuracy of the endogenous microvariables that the actors use as ingredients in their decisionmaking. It seems reasonable, then, to look to the performance of the model when used for projection as a validation of the postdecision behavioral parts of the model. This aspect of the model's performance is examined in chapter 8.

Micromagnitudes and Macromagnitudes

The relation between the microstructure of the model and the simulated macrovariables it produces as output is diagrammed in figure 3.1, which refers to the first quarter of a simulation run. Only one firm and one household are shown. In the top part of the figure, the module creating initial conditions gives as output a vector, $(f_{o,j})$, of the initial values of variables directly affected by decisions of jth firm and a vector, $(h_{o,i})$, of the initial values of variables directly affected by decisions of the ith household. Included in the f vector are items like the price of the firm's product, the wage rates it pays, and the identity of the workers in its employ. Included in the h vector are savings, debt, car and home ownership, and purchases by households of the firms' outputs. In the first round, the firm takes account of the elements relevant to its decisionmaking processes, makes its decision,

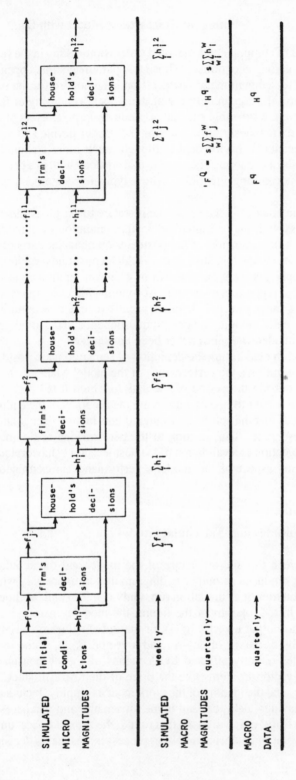

Figure 3.1. Values of Variables Generated in the First Quarter of a Simulation Run (h_i^w, f_i^w = simulated micromagnitudes for the ith actor in the wth week; ${}^\prime H^q$, F^q = simulated macromagnitudes for the qth quarter; H^q, F^q = data on macromagnitudes; s = scale factor)

30

and then engages in the postdecision behavior that produces a new set of elements for the f vector $(f_{1,j})$. The appropriate elements of $h_{o,i}$ and $f_{1,j}$ are next used by households to make their decisions, which together with postdecision behavior results in a new vector $(h_{1,i})$. This process of changing values of microvariables continues round by round. As this is going on, aggregates of some of these simulated microvariables are made on a weekly basis, and these weekly aggregates are futher aggregated through time on a monthly basis (not shown) and a quarterly basis. Monthly aggregations (or averages) are done for variables for which monthly data are available, such as interest rates and number of persons unemployed; quarterly aggregations are made for items in the national income and product accounts and flow-of-funds accounts. The major variables tracked and their average absolute percentage errors of simulation are given in a later chapter (see table 8.1).

The possibilities for errors of simulation in the course of the model's operation are obvious from figure 3.1. Let us assume for the moment that the forms of the decisionmaking equations, the postdecision behavior patterns, and the initial conditions are correct in the sense that a set of parameters exists that permits the tracking of all macrodata series by the simulated macromagnitudes for some predetermined period of time to some predetermined tolerance. Even in this case, the assignment to the parameters of values outside of the set that would by assumption produce the correct result sends the model seriously off track by generating micromagnitudes that are in error and that therefore induce errors in subsequent decisions by the actors. Thus, the representation of short periods of approximately a week, which creates advantages in the representation of economic processes and allows for the elimination of simultaneity, exacts a toll in terms of cumulated errors of simulation. As is discussed below, these cumulated errors of microsimulation also complicate the process of parameter estimation.

The Choice of Estimation Methods

Methodologies for assigning values to the parameters in conventional macroeconomic-equation systems and for making probability statements concerning these parameter estimates have a long history of development. Unfortunately, relatively little attention has been given by econometricians to the development of methodologies that perform the same functions for microsimulation systems.

Nevertheless, a wide variety of methods developed for other contexts can be adapted to simulation models. They vary considerably in the restrictions they place on the form of the model to be estimated. They also vary in the resources they require for implementation. Some methods require armies of researchers to estimate a model the size of this one; others can be effectuated by small groups. Some require large quantities of computer time and real time, while others' requirements in this regard are quite modest.

Fitting to Microdata

Ideally, models that purport to portray actions on the microeconomic level should be fitted to microdata. This is the methodology chosen by Guy Orcutt for the models constructed under his leadership (Orcutt, Caldwell, and Wertheimer 1976). It affords many advantages. Microdata sets, particularly those available for households, contain a vastly greater amount of information than is available from time series, and only with microdata sets is it possible to escape from the colinearity problems of time-series data. Further, microdata sets allow the estimation of nonlinear relationships between microvariables. While nonlinear relationships among macrovariables can be estimated, the application of such relationships to the microlevel is problematical.

Mitigating against a reliance on cross-section microdata is the well-known propensity of models fitted to such data to predict poorly over time. Perhaps even more decisively for the case of the research effort reported here, use of microdata would have required far more resources than were available to the authors.

Full-Information Methods Using Macro Time Series

In fitting to macrodata, search techniques developed for use in engineering design can, at least in principle, be adapted for use in estimating simultaneously all of the parameters of a microsimulated economic model. The first step in implementing such a method is to form an objective function:

$$G = G(H - H_S, F - F_S),$$

where H and H_S represent vectors of actual and simulated macromagnitudes for households, and F and F_S represent vectors of actual and simulated macromagnitudes for firms. Actual values are taken from macrodata. The objective function applies weights to these differences or to functions of them reflecting the researcher's judgment on the relative importance of a good fit to each available data series and to each time period. (For example, the objective function could give more importance to tracking real fixed investment than to tracking price indexes, and more importance to fit in later years than to fit in earlier ones.) The next steps are to assign successive vectors of parameter values to run the model, using each such vector over the period for which one has data, and to evaluate the objective function for that run. A considerable number of schemes have been proposed for deciding how to move from one vector of trial parameter values to another systematically

(Goldfeld and Quandt 1972; Powell 1965). These schemes are designed to maximize the improvement in the objective function for a given number of runs of the model. Of these, the method proposed by Powell (1965) seems most promising for fitting simulation models. This method, which was designed to find the maximum of a function, does not require that the derivatives of the function with respect to the parameters be themselves expressed as functions. It requires for each iteration of its basic procedure a number of runs of the model equal to the number of parameters to be fitted, plus two. Trials of the Powell method with relatively well-behaved functions show that fifty to a hundred iterations may be necessary (Goldfeld and Quandt 1972, 30–37).

The use of search techniques on a full-information basis may prove to be feasible in simulation models with five or fewer parameters to estimate and that take a relatively short time to run through the data period. For the Transactions Model, with its 300 parameters and twenty-minute running time, the use of the Powell techniques seems far out of the question on a full-information basis—even as a second stage, after parsimonious techniques described below have been used to find a starting set of parameter values. The use of search techniques on submodules with few parameters, however, is of greater potential practicality.

Single-Equation Methods Using Time Series

In those cases where (1) it appeared acceptable to specify the microrelationship one wished to estimate as linear, and (2) where all of the variables involved in the equation aggregated to variables available in time-series form (or can be computed from other variables available in time-series form), then linear macroequations estimated with macroeconomic data could be and were used on the microeconomic level. The problem posed by the time aggregation of the macrodata and the model's assumption of weekly decisionmaking was overcome to some extent by interpolation.

Micro/Macro Fitting

Had all the parameter fitting of the model been conducted using macrodata in a conventional manner, it would not be unfair to characterize the model as a fully recursive macromodel, to which a very large superstructure of accounting identities has been added. But we did not want to accept the restrictions on forms of equations and variables a completely conventional method would have required. There were equations where we perceived advantages in using explanatory variables on the microeconomic level for which there was no aggregative equivalent. For these cases—perhaps 10 percent of all equations estimated—we developed a methodology of estimation through the construction of conforming micromagnitudes.

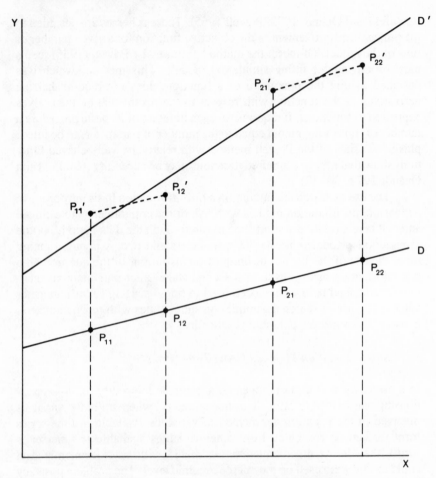

Figure 3.2. Construction of Conforming Micromagnitudes

This process can best be understood with the help of figure 3.2. Consider a single decision process as it is made in two successive rounds of operation of the model by two of the actors represented in the model. The values of the elements in the vector of variables X influence the value that the actors decide to set for variable Y. Variable Y is assumed to have an analog in macroeconomic data, but vector X may contain variables for which there are no such analogs. In the figure, line D' represents an equation that approximates the process decisionmakers use to transform the values of microvariables in X into a decided-upon level for Y. The values of its parameter are correct in the sense defined above—that the macroeconomic analog to Y can be tracked at a predetermined tolerance. These are the parameters whose values we attempt to estimate. Line D represents an equation of the same form, with different numerical values for the parameters. On the first pass through the decision process, let us assume that the values of X have been correctly set in the initial conditions. Using D rather than D', the first and second actors generate points P_{11} and P_{12}, respectively. The macrodata analog to the aggregate of the micro Y values tells us that the values of Y decided on by the actors were not typical of what their real counterparts did in that historical period.

At this point, let us distinguish two modes of running this particular part of the model: an endogenous mode and an exogenous mode. Running in the endogenous mode, no corrections are made of the values of Y, and the run of the model proceeds, incorporating those errors ino the determination of future decisions of all the actors, thereby creating errors in the elements of X, which will be used to determine Y in subsequent rounds. Running in the exogenous mode, by contrast, we correct the values of Y to a certain extent by forcing them to conform in aggregate to the aggregate data. This can be done in a variety of ways; as a first approximation we chose simply to share out the discrepancy proportionally among all the actors, creating points p'_{11} and p'_{12}. To the extent that the values of the parameters controlling the effects of X are in error, the correction will be imperfect, and this will have an effect on the values of the X variables that show up as determinants of the decision in the second round. In any case, the procedure can be repeated round by round, creating points p'_{21} and p'_{22} in round two, and so on. The values of the Y variable created in this process are the conforming micromagnitudes referred to above.

At the end of the run, a regression can be run on all of the p' points as a way of estimating D'. A further refinement would use the information contained in the relation between the size of the correction factor needed to make the Y values conform to the data in a particular round and the average values of the elements in the X vectors in that round. A regression run on those observations can be used to adjust the Y values further, and the estimate of D' can proceed using those corrected values. The entire process can be iterated until it converges.

Implementation Procedures

We chose the 1967–79 period for fitting parameters, using fifty-two observations in each series from the national accounts and the flow-of-funds accounts. Data are available for later years, but these were used only to test the predictive power of the model outside the period of parameter estimation.

All of the information on the basis of which all decisions are made and the results of each decision are kept in the computer memory (COMMON block), which contains full cross-section information at the end of each round. About 43-thousand variables define the positions of all actors at any moment in time. From microdata for the last round in each quarter, we create time series for approximately one fourth of these variables. The resulting set of fifty-two quarterly observations for each series forms the basis of our parameter estimation.

The COMMON blocks that result from the final run of data preparation include the full set of microdata created by running the model in exogenous mode. These are used for several purposes. First, when we later wish to start a run of the model at the beginning of any quarter after 1966, we merely read into the computer the appropriate COMMON block that ends the previous quarter. That COMMON block will contain all of the initial conditions of a run of the model—initial conditions at the exogenous values of the variables matching the history revealed by the data to that point, insofar as is possible.

A second use of the COMMON block resulting from the final exogenous run of the model is to give a standard for comparison of the results of endogenous runs of the model with exogenous runs. If we wish, as we do later, to evaluate the accuracy of model predictions one quarter ahead, the following procedure is followed: (1) read in the exogenous COMMON block ending a quarter, (2) run the model in endogenous mode for the desired equations for twelve rounds, (3) write out the resulting COMMON block, (4) read in the exogenous COMMON block ending the current quarter, and (5) go to (2) and repeat as desired. The resulting time series from the newly written COMMON blocks can be compared with the corresponding exogenous time series to compute statistical information, such as standard errors, for the predictions. If we omit step 4, we can use the resulting COMMON blocks to describe statistically the model errors when they are allowed to accumulate over the entire period of the run, rather than just one quarter. The greater the number of equations we permit to be endogenous in a run of the model, the more we can observe the cumulative effects of interactions among the errors in various of the equations.

Note on Equation Designation

The next four chapters describe the activities of the simulated firms, households, financial institutions, and governments. They contain all of the principal equations the actors use to make decisions, as well as enough examples of the other types of equations in the model to allow the reader to follow the action. We have designated these equations as belonging to four types:

R: Parameters were fitted by linear *regression* to macrodata. These equations are accompanied by average absolute percentage errors for the dependent variable, t-statistics, and $\bar{R}^2$ values.

I: Parameters were derived by an *iterative* process using macrodata.

E: Numerical values of the parameters were derived *extraneously*. They include periods of production and ratios, which reconcile published estimates of components with published estimates of sums and reconcile data from divergent sources. Many of these parameters are simple averages or ratios.

A: These equations display the *accounting* consequences of decisionmaking and usually have no parameters.

In the text of the next four chapters, the parameters are denoted by lower-case italic letters in the equations. Each equation, with its parameter values, t-statistic, average absolute percentage error, and $\bar{R}^2$ value, is presented in the appendix. In each equation, a (1) is the first parameter, a (2) the second, and so on. Naturally, the numerical values differ for each equation.

Chapter 4. The Firms

A firm's history is the history of its decisions, its attempts to translate those decisions into actions, and the physical and financial results to it of its own actions and the actions of all of the other actors. In this chapter we describe our treatment of the decisionmaking and resultant actions of firms with respect to production, inventory accumulation, hiring and layoffs, purchases from other firms, pricing of output, setting wages and hours, and paying taxes. A treatment of the firm's activities with respect to fixed investment, debt service, debt creation, portfolio management, and dividend payments is also included. The activities peculiar to the two firms specializing in financial services are dealt with in chapter 6.

In a microsimulated model such as the Transactions Model, the firm is a collection of numerical magnitudes that display its characteristics, its possibilities, and its situation and history. The magnitudes pertaining to each firm, are continually updated as the model runs and are used by the firm in the course of its decisionmaking.[1] They define the firm's production possibilities and its materials and labor requirements; they provide ingredients for the firm's profit-and-loss statement and its balance sheet. Table 4.1 describes this information with its computer codes.

This chapter is organized in the sequence in which events occur as the model runs. The preparation of the data used to estimate parameters and the methods used in setting up the initial microconditions are discussed in notes. As explained at the end of chapter 3, parameter values are presented in the appendix.

The Production Setup

A physical unit of a firm's output is defined as that amount of output that sold for one dollar in 1972. To produce output, the firm uses stocks of capital goods called machines; labor, which cooperates with the capital goods; and material inputs, which are purchased from other firms and consumed in the production process.

Each machine has a rated capacity to produce physical output, and the production of a unit of the firm's output utilizes one unit of the capacity of a machine. A machine is defined as an assemblage of physical goods from up to eight of the firms worth one dollar in total in 1972. Machines are differentiated by age; a machine of a more recent vintage consists physically of an assemblage of the same goods as an older machine but requires less labor per unit of output. This change in the characteristics of new machines represents embodied technical change. Machines last fifteen years and an improved group of machines appears at the beginning of each quarter, so at any time a firm has sixty vintages of machines available for production. There is no deterioration in a machine's output capacity or labor requirements as time passes; on the contrary, disembodied technical change is represented as a change through time in the amount a machine produces when combined with a fixed quantity of labor.[2]

The amounts of material inputs from other firms required as a flow per physical unit of output are derived from the 1972 input/output table and are assumed not to vary over time and not to depend on the vintage or characteristics of the machine used to produce that unit. A final physical necessity for production is the maintenance of a central-office staff, whose size does not vary with output but changes through time. We call it the fixed staff and the rest the variable staff.

Production Planning in the Short Run

Production planning is based on the assumption that the firm is willing to produce and sell all that it can at the price it sets. Certain firms, notably those that produce services, do not maintain inventories of their own product but produce to order.[3] They produce and deliver in one round what their customers have ordered and paid for in the previous round. If shortages of labor, capital, or materials prevent firms from filling orders, unfilled orders are backlogged and produced at the first opportunity.

Domestic firms producing inventoried goods (agriculture, mining, automobile manufacturing, other durable manufacturing, nondurable manufacturing, and trade) sell to households and governments out of inventories. They deal with other firms on the basis of orders. Five rounds are required between an order and the finish of delivery of a product that is not a fixed-capital good. For fixed-capital goods, the period from order to the end of delivery is thirty rounds (Grebler and Maisel 1963; Bosworth and Duesenberry 1974). Each round a goods-producing firm delivers to other firms one-thirtieth of the real value of the fixed-capital projects it has started previously but not delivered, and one-fifth of other orders it has not filled.

Production plans are conditioned by the firm's desire to maintain an inventory of its own output to cushion erratic changes in sales. The produc-

Table 4.1. Information available concerning each fictional firm

Inputs to production

AIO(JFIRM,IFIRM):	Physical units of the product of JFIRM required as input for the production of one unit of the product of IFIRM. (Unchanging)
AIOCAP(JFIRM, IFIRM):	Units of output of JFIRM required to put in place a new machine for the use of IFIRM. (Unchanging)
DESEMP(IFIRM):	Number of variable employees desired by IFIRM.
EMP(IFIRM):	Total current employment by IFIRM.
EMPFIX(IFIRM):	Number of employees on the fixed staff.
FLABOR(ICASTE,IFIRM):	Proportion of EMPFIX(IFIRM) required to be of occupation ICASTE.
HRS(IFIRM):	Ratio of weekly hours to standard workweek.
LVIN(IFIRM):	Marginal vintage of machines currently required to produce AVSALE(IFIRM).
ONEW(IFIRM):	Output producible with one unit of new machine.
OPUT(IFIRM,JVIN):	Output producible in a week on all of the machines of vintage JVIN if workers are on a standard workweek.
RLAB(IFIRM,JVIN):	Number of IFIRM employees required to cooperate with all machines of vintage JVIN.
RLABOR(ICASTE,IFIRM):	Proportion of DESEMP(IFIRM) required to be of occupation ICASTE.
STARTM(IFIRM):	Backlog of IFIRM's orders for machines.
XLNEW(IFIRM):	Labor required to cooperate with one unit of new machines.

Production, sales, and inventories

AVSALE(IFIRM):	Geometrically weighted moving average of SALE(IFIRM).
CAPCY(IFIRM):	Maximum currently available capacity for output.
CAPSHT(IFIRM):	Desired output not produced because of capacity shortage.
DINV(IFIRM):	Inventory of its own product desired by IFIRM.
DPROD(IFIRM):	Current weekly desired production.
ORDERS(JFIRM,IFIRM):	Backlog of IFIRM's orders for JFIRM's product.
PINV(JFIRM,IFIRM):	Inventory of JFIRM's product held by IFIRM just after the once-a-round addition to stocks from purchase or production.
SALE(IFIRM):	Current weekly sales in physical units.
SALEIN(IFIRM):	Current weekly interindustry sales in physical units.
SHORT(IFIRM):	Quantity of product demanded but not sold in current week because of inventory deficiency.
SHPROD(IFIRM):	Difference between desired and actual production.
XINV(JFIRM,IFIRM):	Quantity of JFIRM's product held by IFIRM as inventory.
XPROD(IFIRM):	Actual production in the current week.

Costs, prices, and profits

ACOST(IFIRM):	Average cost of units of output currently produced.
AVGDIV(IFIRM):	Geometrically weighted moving average of corporate dividends of IFIRM (at a weekly rate).
AVPCH(IFIRM):	Geometrically weighted moving average of relative change in P(IFIRM).
CAPCO(IFIRM):	Weekly capital consumption allowances of IFIRM.
CPMARG(IFIRM):	Current profit margin over average cost.
P(IFIRM):	Current price (including indirect tax) of IFIRM's product.
PI(IFIRM):	Acquisition price of the average unit of IFIRM's current inventory.
PLAST(IFIRM)	Price of IFIRM's output in last period.
PMACH(IFIRM):	Current cost of a machine purchased by IFIRM.
PMARG(IFIRM):	Geometrically weighted moving average of CPMARG(IFIRM).
PROFIT(IFIRM):	Profits on current week's output.

Table 4.1. *(continued)*

PRTAX(IFIRM):	Current period's payroll-tax liability.
TCOST:	Total weekly cost of production.
WAGE(IFIRM):	Current weekly wage of IFIRM's average worker.
WAGEF(ICASTE,IFIRM):	Weekly wage paid by IFIRM to average worker in occupation ICASTE.
XINTER(IFIRM):	Weekly interest paid by IFIRM, net of interest received.
XMCOST(IFIRM):	Marginal cost at current level of output.
Financial assets and liabilities	
BBONDS(IFIRM):	Maturity value of long-term securities held by IFIRM.
BILLS(IFIRM):	Maturity value of treasury bills held by IFIRM.
BLOANS(IFIRM,IMAT):	Bank loans to IFIRM maturing in week IMAT.
BONDS(IFIRM,IMAT):	Maturity value of outstanding bonds issued by IFIRM and maturing in month IMAT.
CASH(IFIRM):	Demand deposits held by IFIRM.

tion-planning process starts by computing sales in the last round based on the change in inventory over the period:

$$\text{SALE(IFIRM)} = \text{PINV(IFIRM,IFIRM)} - \text{XINV(IFIRM,IFIRM)}, \qquad (4.1)$$

whose magnitudes are defined above.

The firm next considers the level of inventories it wishes to hold of its own good and of the goods of other firms. It computes the desired ratio of inventories to its own weekly sales as a function of the difference between a moving average of the relative weekly price change of the inventoried product, AVPCH(JFIRM), and the cost of holding the inventory, represented by the current treasury-bill rate on a weekly basis, RBILL(12), and TIME:[4]

$$\text{DIN(JFIRM,IFIRM)} = a(1) + a(2)*[\text{AVPCH(JFIRM)} - \text{RBILL}(12)] \\ + a(3)*\text{TIME}. \qquad (4.2)$$

The firm then computes desired inventories as

$$\text{DINV(JFIRM,IFIRM)} = \text{DIN(JFIRM,IFIRM)}*\text{AVSALE(IFIRM)} \qquad (4.3) \\ *\text{AIO(JFIRM,IFIRM)},$$

where AVSALE is a moving average of SALE, and the AIO are input/output coefficients. The value of AIO is one if JFIRM is equal to IFIRM.

The firm then adds to the outstanding orders for its own product and the products of other firms. It updates ORDERS(JFIRM,IFIRM):[5]

$$\text{ORDERS(JFIRM,IFIRM)} = \text{ORDERS(JFIRM,IFIRM)}_o \qquad (4.4) \\ + a(1)*[\text{DINV(JFIRM,IFIRM)} - \text{PINV(JFIRM,IFIRM)}] \\ + \text{SALE(IFIRM)}*\text{AIO(JFIRM,IFIRM)},$$

where the subscript o indicates the level of the variable set previously. The firm then determines its desired quantity of production for the current round:

$$\text{DPROD(IFIRM)} = a(1)*\text{ORDERS(IFIRM,IFIRM)}, \qquad (4.5)$$

if the firm holds inventories. Otherwise,

$$\text{DPROD(IFIRM)} = \text{SALE(IFIRM)}. \tag{4.5'}$$

The firm next checks for feasibility of the selected output target. One constraint is due to capacity limitations:

$$\text{DPROD(IFIRM)} = MIN[\text{CAPCY(IFIRM)}, \text{DPROD(IFIRM)}_o], \tag{4.6}$$

where CAPCY is the maximum output the capital stock can produce at maximum permissible weekly hours. Another constraint relates to the firm's inventories of material inputs:

$$\text{DPROD(IFIRM)} = MIN[\text{XINV(JFIRM,IFIRM)}/\text{AIO(JFIRM,IFIRM)}, \tag{4.7}$$
$$\text{DPROD(IFIRM)}_o].$$

If either of these constraints is unsatisfied, targeted production will be reduced.

Employment and Hours Decisions

Having set its desired output, the firm now decides upon the number of employees to have on board in the current round. It is cognizant of the fact that a change in the number of employees—in either direction—will result in wasteful expenditure if it must be reversed, so that sudden (and possibly reversible) shifts in the quantity of production are avoided by relatively slow and deliberate changes in the size of the staff. Changes in the length of the workweek contribute to the short-run adjustment process. However, the firm also recognizes that when weekly hours exceed the standard workweek, overtime premiums are incurred, and when weekly hours are lower than standard, hourly costs rise because of fixed per-employee costs and employee dissatisfaction.[6] Consequently, when output is stable or changing only slowly, a firm moves its weekly hours back toward the standard workweek. In any case, it sets a ceiling on and a floor under weekly hours.

The firm's cognizance of the costs and benefits of changing output, employment, and hours is implemented by having it (1) tentatively move weekly hours nearer to the standard workweek, (2) figure the employees it needs to achieve production targets at these weekly hours, and (3) readjust employment and weekly hours if necessary within specified limits. If the firm bumps up against a self-imposed ceiling in both hiring and hours, it will produce less than it wants to for a time. If it encounters a floor, it will produce more. We set the initial adjustments of HRS(IFIRM) (the ratio of actual weekly hours to standard weekly hours) as a fraction of the current overtime or undertime:[7]

$$\text{HRS(IFIRM)} = \text{HRS(IFIRM)}_o + a(1)*[1 - \text{HRS(IFIRM)}_o]. \tag{4.8}$$

The firm next determines the size of the variable staff needed to produce DPROD(IFIRM) with HRS(IFIRM) as tentatively set. It allows for the fact that disembodied technical change results in more output from each vintage of machines than in the previous period:[8]

$$\text{OPUT(IFIRM,JVIN)} = [1 + a\text{(IFIRM)}]*\text{OPUT(IFIRM,JVIN)}_o. \qquad (4.9)$$

Since the youngest vintages of capital produce with the least labor and therefore at least cost, it will use the youngest vintages of capital to full capacity, using as few vintages as possible. The firm finds values of LVIN (the marginal vintage) and Z (the fraction of the marginal-vintage machines used) such that

$$\sum_{\text{JVIN}=1}^{\text{LVIN}-1} \text{OPUT(IFIRM,JVIN)}*\text{HRS(IFIRM)} \qquad (4.10)$$
$$+ \text{OPUT(IFIRM,LVIN)}*\text{HRS(IFIRM)}*\text{Z} = \text{DPROD(IFIRM)}.$$

The firm finds LVIN and Z by using a simple algorithm that cumulates output in successive vintages, starting with the youngest and stopping when the output target is reached. Once the values of LVIN and Z associated with DPROD(IFIRM) are known, the firm can straightforwardly compute the variable labor required, by

$$\text{TLAB} = \sum_{\text{JVIN}=1}^{\text{LVIN}-1} \text{RLAB(IFIRM,JVIN)} + \text{Z}*\text{RLAB(IFIRM,LVIN)}. \qquad (4.11)$$

Finally, the firm adjusts the desired level of its fixed staff by[9]

$$\text{EMPFIX(IFIRM)} = a\text{(IFIRM)} + b\text{(IFIRM)}*\text{TIME}. \qquad (4.12)$$

Hiring Hall Operation

The first event in the operation of the hiring hall is that some persons enter the labor force and some unemployed persons leave the labor force. Second, randomly chosen workers quit their jobs at a rate linearly related to the unemployment rate. The processes controlling both of these events are described in chapter 5.

Next, the firm hires or lays off workers to fulfill its production plans for the round. The workers available for employment are in one of four occupations (see Table 2.1). In periods of labor shortage, mobility among occupations is permitted. The firm's demand for persons of a given occupation depends on the sizes of the fixed and variable staffs it currently requires and the distribution of these staffs by occupation. The total demand for employees by occupation is computed by

$$\text{SUMD(ICASTE)} = \text{EMPFIX(IFIRM)} * \text{FLABOR(ICASTE,IFIRM)} \qquad \textbf{(4.13)}$$
$$+ \text{DESEMP(IFIRM)} * \text{RLABOR(ICASTE,IFIRM)},$$

where RLABOR(ICASTE,IFIRM) and FLABOR(ICASTE,IFIRM) are, respectively, the proportions of IFIRM's variable and fixed staffs in occupation ICASTE.[10]

The total quantity of employed labor by all firms (plus that employed by the governments) must meet the constraints

$$\text{EMPC(ICASTE)} \leq a(1) * \text{SLABOR(ICASTE)}, \qquad \textbf{(4.14)}$$

where SLABOR(ICASTE) is the number of persons currently in the labor force in occupation ICASTE. If these constraints are not met, the firm will fail to fill its hiring goal and may react by raising weekly hours and possibly lowering production from the level planned.[11] If there is a shortage of labor in one occupation, the firm will scale down its demands for labor in all other occupations, so as to maintain the distribution of staffs described in the FLABOR and RLABOR arrays.

Next, the firm hires or lays off workers to bring actual employment, after accounting for quits, into line with desired employment, SUMD—scaled down if necessary. If layoffs are called for, employed workers of appropriate occupation are chosen at random to be laid off, and these workers become unemployed. If hiring is called for, the firm offers jobs to randomly encountered unemployed workers at a wage for a standard work-week, the wage being specific to the firm and to the occupation and skill level of the worker. (See below for description of wage setting by firms.) The worker's acceptance depends on the offered wage, the amount of time the worker has been unemployed, and his or her eligibility for unemployment insurance. If there is an excessive number of refusals or if there is a shortage of labor, each firm's employment level falls short of that desired.

After the close of the labor market, the firm computes the physical output, X, that can be produced with the labor it now has on board at the tentatively set weekly hours. Hours are now reset to

$$\text{HRS(IFIRM)} = \text{HRS(IFIRM)}_o * \text{DPROD(IFIRM)}/\text{X}, \qquad \textbf{(4.15)}$$

subject to the constraint[12]

$$[1 - a(1)] < \text{HRS(IFIRM)} < [1 + a(1)], \qquad \textbf{(4.16)}$$

and slated production is now reset by

$$\text{XPROD(IFIRM)} = \text{X} * \text{HRS(IFIRM)}/\text{HRS(IFIRM)}_o. \qquad \textbf{(4.17)}$$

Wage Setting

Average basic wages for a standard workweek are changed each round by each firm for each occupation:

$$\text{WAGEF(ICASTE,IFIRM)} = \text{WAGEF(ICASTE,IFIRM)}_o \qquad \textbf{(4.18)}$$
$$*[1 + a(1) + a(2)*\text{CPICH} + a(3)*\text{PRODCH}],$$

where CPICH is the change in the consumer price index over the past six months and PRODCH is the change in the output per worker over the last quarter (Schultze and Tryon 1965).

Production and the Management of Inventories

Production of an amount X in a goods-producing firm takes the form of an addition to the firm's inventory of its own output:

$$\text{XINV(IFIRM,IFIRM)} = \text{XINV(IFIRM,IFIRM)}_o + \text{X}. \qquad \textbf{(4.19)}$$

Production requires the consumption of materials inputs consisting of the outputs of other firms, represented by a drawing down of the inventories the firm keeps of those outputs:

$$\text{XINV(JFIRM,IFIRM)} = \text{XINV(JFIRM,IFIRM)}_o \qquad \textbf{(4.20)}$$
$$- \text{X}*\text{AIO(JFIRM,IFIRM)},$$

where the AIO are input/output coefficients.

Cost and Profit Accounting

The firm now computes its sales receipts, the cost of goods sold (on a LIFO basis), its inventory adjustment, and its profits. Total cost, TCOST, is the sum of a number of components:

$$\text{Materials cost} = \text{XMATC} = \sum_{\text{JFIRM}} \text{P(JFIRM)}*\text{AIO(JFIRM,IFIRM)}*\text{X}. \qquad \textbf{(4.21)}$$

$$\text{Fixed-staff cost} = \sum_{\text{ICASTE}} \text{EMPFIX(IFIRM)}*\text{FLABOR(ICASTE,IFIRM)} \qquad \textbf{(4.22)}$$
$$*\text{WAGEF(ICASTE,IFIRM)}.$$

$$\text{Variable-staff cost} = \sum_{\text{ICASTE}} \text{DESEMP(IFIRM)} \qquad \textbf{(4.23)}$$
$$*\text{RLABOR(ICASTE,IFIRM)}*\text{WAGEF(ICASTE,IFIRM)}*\text{X}.$$

Also included are payroll tax on fixed and variable staffs, interest charges on the firm's outstanding liabilities, capital-consumption allowances based on an accelerated straight-line method applied to total book value, which changes when investment is made, and business transfer payments. Average cost of goods produced is computed

$$\text{ACOST(IFIRM)} = \text{TCOST}/\text{X}, \tag{4.24}$$

while marginal cost is computed

$$\text{XMCOST(IFIRM)} = \frac{\text{XLABCO(IFIRM)}}{\text{DESEMP(IFIRM)}} \tag{4.25}$$

$$* \frac{\text{RLAB(IFIRM,LVIN)}}{\text{OPUT(IFIRM,LVIN)}*\text{HRS(IFIRM)}}$$

$$- \frac{\text{XMATC}}{\text{X}},$$

where LVIN is as before the marginal vintage, and XLABCO(IFIRM) is the sum of variable-staff wage costs and the payroll tax on this staff.

Profits are figured as

$$\text{PROFIT(IFIRM)} = \text{SALE(IFIRM)}*\text{P(IFIRM)}*(1 - \text{TAXIND(IFIRM)})$$

$$- \text{TCOST}*\text{SALE(IFIRM)}/\text{X}, \tag{4.26}$$

where TAXIND(IFIRM) is the average rate of indirect business tax on IFIRM's product.

In figure 4.1 we have traced out the simulated average and marginal cost curves for the last round of the last quarter of 1979 of firm 5, other durable manufacturing. On the horizontal axis, weekly output is measured in physical units, one unit being that amount of product that sold for one dollar in 1972. The figure also shows a point representing the weekly sales level and the price simulated for the last quarter of 1979. At this level of sales, the elasticity of average cost with respect to output is -0.17. The profit per dollar of sales is $0.025. For this firm, the minimum point of the average cost curve is reached at the forty-fifth vintage.

Dividend Distribution

For each industry, profits are divided into a corporate fraction, CORP(IFIRM), on which corporate taxes are paid, and a noncorporate fraction. Corporate dividends are paid from the after-tax profits:[13]

$$\text{DIV} = a(1)*\text{PROFIT(IFIRM)}*[1 - \text{POL}(8) - \text{POL}(10)]*\text{CORP(IFIRM)}$$

$$+ a(2)*\text{AVGDIV(IFIRM)}, \tag{4.27}$$

where AVGDIV(IFIRM) is a moving average of IFIRM's corporate dividends and POL(8) and POL(10) are the federal corporate-tax rate and the average of state/local tax rates, respectively. Corporate dividends are sent to the financial intermediary, which pools the dividend payments from all firms and distributes them to households in proportion to their equity holdings.

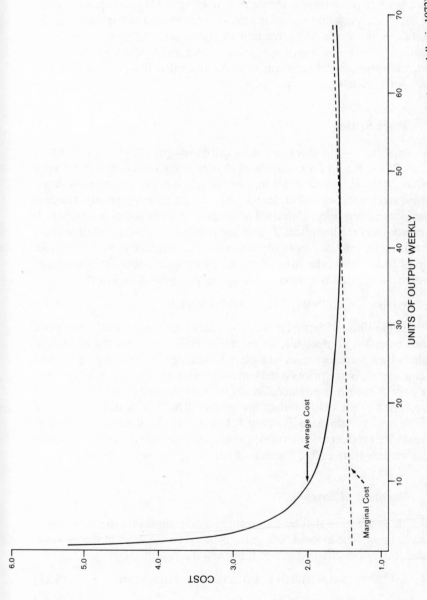

Figure 4.1. Cost Curves of the Other Durable Manufacturing Firm, Last Quarter of 1979 (one output unit sold for one dollar in 1972)

47

Noncorporate profits are treated somewhat differently. If profits are positive, a fraction is distributed through the financial intermediary to households in proportion to their equity holdings.[14] If noncorporate profits are negative, households owning equities are required to contribute equity capital, equal to the same fraction of the losses, through the financial intermediary to those firms having losses. Households balance losses from a particular firm against subsequent profits from that firm, without limit of time, for personal-tax computation.

Price Setting

The steps that a firm takes to decide price changes are outlined in figure 4.2.[15] Prices are up for endogenous change every round, except for agriculture, mining, the financial intermediary, the bank, government enterprises, and the rest-of-world, for which prices are set exogenously. The firm considers raising prices if desired production exceeds actual production. It also considers raising prices if marginal cost exceeds price (net of indirect taxes) or if the current profit margin is below the customary profit margin. In any of these cases, the firm raises prices by a firm-specific percentage, AVPCH(IFIRM), that is a moving average of past price changes:[16]

$$P(IFIRM) = P(IFIRM)_o * [1 + AVPCH(IFIRM)]. \tag{4.28}$$

In the 1967–79 period to which the parameters were fitted, most price series recorded no declines, so empirical evidence about the conditions under which declines would take place is lacking. The firm is programmed to consider reducing prices if the current profit margin is above the customary one. A firm that produces an inventoried product lowers the price if inventories of its own product are greater than 111 percent of desired inventories, as defined in equation 4.3.[17] A firm that does not produce an inventoried product assesses the trend of its sales and lowers price if current sales are less than a fixed fraction of a moving average of its sales.[18]

Payment of Taxes

Sales taxes are collected by the firm from households on the occasion of sales to them. The amount forwarded is based on the sales of the previous round, the prices charged at that time, and the rate of taxation:

$$SALTAX = SALE(IFIRM)*PLAST(IFIRM)*TAXIND(IFIRM). \tag{4.29}$$

The firm sends a share to the federal government and the remainder to the state/local government. Payroll taxes previously computed on this round's wages are sent to the federal government. Corporate-profits taxes are paid to the federal government:

$$PROTAX = CORP(IFIRM)*PROFIT(IFIRM)*POL(8), \tag{4.30}$$

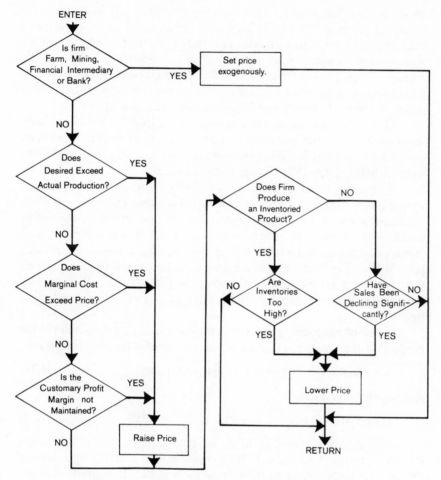

Figure 4.2. Sequence of Decisionmaking on Price Changes

where CORP(IFIRM) is the proportion of the firm's computed profits that count as corporate profits as defined for tax purposes, and POL(8) is a policy instrument whose value is set by the federal government. If PROTAX is less than zero, the loss can be used to offset future profits for tax purposes without limit of time. Corporate taxes are also paid to the state/local government at a tax rate POL(10) on a similar basis.

Investment in Nonresidential Fixed Capital

The firm's decisions on how many physical units of fixed capital goods to order are dependent on eight sets of magnitudes: (1) rate of interest on bonds, AVRBON; (2) prices in industries whose output includes components of capital goods, P(JFIRM); (3) labor requirements and output capacity of existing capital stock, RLAB(IFIRM,JVIN) and OPUT(IFIRM,JVIN); (4) cost per worker on the variable staff, XLABCO(IFIRM)/DESEMP(IFIRM); (5) moving average of sales, AVSALE(IFIRM); (6) loss of capacity due to scrappage; (7) rate of change in the labor requirements and output capacity of new capital goods, a(IFIRM), b(IFIRM); and (8) investment tax credit, if any.

Other factors cited in the literature as statistically associated with investment levels, such as cash flow and prices in equity markets, tend to be correlated with items in the list above but are not included directly. (Meyer and Kuh 1957; Coen 1971; Evans 1969, 124–25).

At the beginning of each quarter, the firms whose output includes capital-goods components make available to each firm a new and improved vintage of machine specialized to the use of that firm. In each of the twelve rounds of the quarter, each firm orders capital equipment currently being produced. It cannot order capital equipment like that produced in previous periods. However, the speed and nature of technological change are such that, at current prices for capital goods, no firm wishes to buy an old-fashioned machine, regardless of the wage rate or of the prices of other inputs.

A unit of machinery produced in the current quarter cooperates in the production of more output than a machine produced in the previous quarter:

$$\text{ONEW(IFIRM)} = \text{ONEW(IFIRM)}_o * [1 + a(\text{IFIRM})], \tag{4.31}$$

and requires less labor:

$$\text{XLNEW(IFIRM)} = \text{XLNEW(IFIRM)}_o * [1 + a(\text{IFIRM})]. \tag{4.32}$$

The rates of embodied technological change represented in the parameters of equations 4.31 and 4.32 are among the most crucial magnitudes of the model. On them depend not only investment but productivity change, labor requirements, and cost trends. The method we used in estimating them is iterative, which finds parameter values that minimize errors of output prediction.

Since we assume that materials inputs per unit of output are not affected by the technological change in machine characteristics, and since the labor costs of producing a unit of output on a new machine are less than that on any previously produced machine, a new machine has lower running costs than any machine from a previous vintage. In considering whether to purchase a new machine, the firm balances the savings derived from the lower running cost of the new machine against the costs incurred in its acquisition (Lutz and Lutz 1951, 112–14).

The savings in running cost occurs because the new machine produces output that would have been produced on a less-efficient machine, which is now unused as a result of the acquisition of the new machine.[19] In calculating the cost savings, it is necessary to pinpoint just which machine is replaced. A firm anticipating producing at the same level as in the recent past takes machines out of production in order of vintage, starting with the oldest, LVIN(IFIRM). A higher anticipated production rate suggests that the cost comparison be made with machines in older vintages than the ones in LVIN(IFIRM). A lower anticipated production rate suggests a comparison with machines of more recent vintages. Since we assume better labor productivity for newer machines, the older the machine whose labor costs are compared with the labor costs of a new machine, the more advantageous the new machine will be by comparison. Thus the investment-decision rule we are using makes the anticipated rate of production (for which the moving average of the current rate is used as a proxy) an important variable in the determination of the investment rate, a formulation in line with empirical studies of investment behavior (Evans 1969, chapter 5).

The labor cost of running all the machines in vintage JVIN = LVIN(IFIRM) for one round depends on the number of workers the vintage requires and the cost per worker on the variable staff:

$$LCO = RLAB(IFIRM,JVIN) * \frac{XLABCO(IFIRM)}{DESEMP(IFIRM)}. \tag{4.33}$$

The labor cost of running a single new machine is

$$LCN = XLNEW(IFIRM) * \frac{XLABCO(IFIRM)}{DESEMP(IFIRM)}. \tag{4.34}$$

To the latter must be added the acquisition costs of the new machine. For a single machine we calculate per-round depreciation as[20]

$$DEP = \sum_{JFIRM} [AIOCAP(JFIRM,IFIRM)*P(FJIRM)]/336.7, \tag{4.35}$$

and the interest cost per round as

$$RCOST = a(1) * \frac{AVRBON}{48} * \sum_{JFIRM} AIOCAP(JFIRM,IFIRM)*P(JFIRM), \tag{4.36}$$

where AVRBON is a moving average of the annual rate of interest on newly issued government bonds.[21] (The firm uses a moving average rather than the volatile current rate because it finances machines as they are delivered rather than as they are ordered.)

The firm considers it advantageous to produce on newly purchased machines the output currently produced on machines of JVIN if[22]

$$\frac{OPUT(IFIRM,JVIN)}{ONEW(IFIRM)} * (LCN + DEP + RCOST) < a(IFIRM)*LCO. \tag{4.37}$$

If the firm's calculations indicate that it would be advantageous to replace the machines of vintage LVIN(IFIRM), it makes the same calculation for the next younger vintage, and goes on in this way until it reaches a

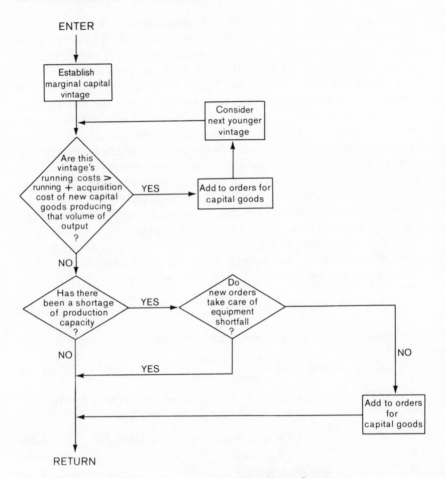

Figure 4.3.   Sequence of Decisionmaking on Investment

vintage not worth replacing, arriving at XMBUY(IFIRM), the cost-effective number of machines to order in the current round. This investment-decision process is shown diagramatically in figure 4.3.

The investing firm then updates its backlog of orders for fixed nonresidential capital by distributing appropriately scaled orders among the firms that produce capital-goods components. The capital-producing firms backlog these orders and deliver each round to the investing firms an amount equal to one-thirtieth of the order backlog.

While the placing of new orders is a move by the firm to improve the characteristics of that part of its capital used to produce output, the orders also increase total capacity to produce if the output capacity of the new equipment is greater than the output capacity of that part of sixtieth-vintage equipment decommissioned in the current round. The firm computes its change in capacity for the round resulting from its new deliveries of capital, BUY, as[23]

$$\text{CHCAP} = a(1)*[\text{BUY}*\text{ONEW(IFIRM)} \qquad\qquad (4.38)$$
$$- \text{OPUT(IFIRM, } 60)/(13 - \text{WEEK})],$$

where WEEK is the number of the current week in the current quarter.

Investment in Residential Property by the Real-Estate Firm

The real-estate firm maintains stocks of real property that have been produced for the most part by the construction industry. Part of this stock consists of nonresidential real property, whose services are rented to other industries in amounts dictated by the input/output table. Another part of the real-estate firm's stock consists of dwelling units whose services are rented to nonhomeowning households. Finally, part of the stock of residential housing in the possession of the real-estate firm is destined for sale to households who are either changing from renters to owners or are exchanging the homes they currently own for differently sized ones.

The real-estate firm operates much like the other firms in its production, inventory, and investment decisions; that is, it tries to gear its operations closely to the amount of goods and services its customers wish to buy at the current price. However, part of the newly produced housing it buys from the construction firm is an investment good, whose purpose is the production of real-estate services for sale, while another part is inventory, from which sales of the housing units themselves are made.

Our treatment of household demand for buying or renting dwelling units is discussed in detail in chapter 5. In brief, decisions on the purchase of homes and automobiles, unlike other purchases, are shown as directly sensitive to interest rates. Home purchasing is also more sensitive to unemployment rates, and households with a member in the work force who is unemployed are programmed not to initiate dwelling-unit purchases.

Sales of new housing to final demand (that is, sale of housing to households by the real-estate firm and the firm's acquisition of rental housing) are financed in the model through loans secured by mortgages. Thus the availability of mortgage money is a constraint on the number of units the real-estate firm orders from the construction firm to meet the demands of its customers. (Grebler and Maisel 1963; Gramlich and Jaffee 1972; Bosworth and Duesenberry 1974).

The real-estate firm in each round orders physical units of housing which take thirty rounds to build.[24] Before placing its orders initiating housing starts, it collects commitments from the bank and the financial intermediary for mortgage financing for thirty rounds hence. These commitments constitute an upper bound on its start orders. The availability of mortgage money is very closely tied to the growth of savings deposits and the asset portfolio of the bank. These and the other factors that condition the availability of mortgage money are discussed below.

The mortgage funds (MFUNDS) committed by the financial institutions are translated into physical units of housing by

$$\text{COMMIT} = \text{MFUNDS}*(1 - \text{PDOWN})/\text{HOMPRI}, \tag{4.39}$$

where PDOWN is the proportion of the value of a house paid in a down payment (controlled by the monetary authority), and HOMPRI is the average price of the construction, durables, and so on, that make up a housing unit.

Adjusting the Portfolio

The activities during the round of the firm, its customers, debtors, creditors, and the government result in a change in the quantity and composition of the firm's assets and liabilities:

1. Cash flows in through sales of its product and receipt of interest payments on its financial assets; cash flows out to purchase the output of other firms and to pay wages, taxes, dividends, and interest on bank loans and bonded indebtedness.
2. Inventory changes through production and sales.
3. Fixed capital used in production changes due to retirement and new purchases.
4. New bank loans are taken out to make necessary transactions when ready cash is not on hand.
5. Three firms—the bank, the financial intermediary, and trade— acquire a share of the debt instruments consumers create in the current round.[25]

The last actions of each firm during the round are to pay off obligations that are due, collect payment on obligations of others, and adjust the quantities of its assets and liabilities to achieve a comfortable liquidity position for the start of the next round.

A firm starts this process by floating long-term bond issues, with a maturity of fifteen years, in an amount proportional to the fixed capital purchases made in the current round:[26]

$$\text{BONSEL} = a(1)*\text{CAPBUY}(\text{JFIRM},\text{IFIRM})*\text{P}(\text{JFIRM}). \tag{4.40}$$

Next the firm pays off long-term bonds and bank loans that are due, .25* BONDS(IFIRM, 1) and BLOANS(IFIRM, 1), respectively, and receives cash for a proportion of its holdings of others' obligations, BBONDS(IFIRM) and BILLS(IFIRM), equal to the share of all such obligations coming due in the current round. The firm next looks at its financial assets: cash, government bills, and longer-term open-market securities issued by the other sectors.[27]

The firm decides on the total financial assets it wishes to maintain and their allocation among the assets. Changes in the firm's financial assets during the round were governed by the cash flow generated by the firm's ordinary operations. If this flow resulted in an unsatisfactory stock of financial assets, the firm changes the stock of its bank loans to bring its financial assets to the desired level.

The model's firms have access at any time during the round to bank loans if they need to raise cash for the purpose of making a purchase. One might well then ask why these firms maintain additional liabilities to the bank, on which they must pay relatively high interest in order to keep a portfolio of financial assets. There are two answers, one relating to the real world and the other to the exigencies of building models of this sort.

In the real world, firms maintain portfolios of financial assets financed by liabilities to banks to maintain flexibility and to limit the bank's decision-making power over their day-to-day operations. In the model, moreover, the single firm in each industry is a composite of firms, some of which have large bank loans and small asset portfolios and some of which have small bank loans and large portfolios. Thus, a firm in the model, if it is to follow the flow-of-funds accounts, has a balance sheet with larger assets and larger liabilities than a profit-maximizing firm in the real world would want.

In fitting to flow-of-funds data, we estimate the firm's desire for liquid assets to be a function of physical volume of sales, AVSALE, the price of the firm's product, P(IFIRM), and the current interest rate for bank loans, RBLO:

$$\text{TFASTS} = \text{AVSALE(IFIRM)} * \text{P(IFIRM)} \qquad (4.41)$$
$$* [a(1) + a(2) * \text{RBLO} + a(3) * \text{TIME}].$$

The firm now adjusts its desired stock of financial assets by increasing or decreasing its bank loans. It then allocates its portfolio among cash, treasury bills, and bonds, which are shares in the total stock of bonds issued by all of the actors in the model. It does this by calculating weights for each

Table 4.2. Parameters of demand for financial assets, nonfinacncial firms

Asset	Intercept	Return	Change in Return	Time	AAPE[a]	$\bar{R}^2$
Cash	0.6713			−0.00045	5.08	.85
	(68.6)			(−17.1)		
Treasury bills	0.0754	−0.7683		+0.000011	119	.39
	(9.383)	−(5.42)		(0.778)		
Bonds	−0.0568	−12.50	+0.829	+0.001033	6.21	.89
	(−0.736)	(−5.73)	(5.96)	(10.3)		

NOTE: *t*-statistics are in parentheses.
[a]Average absolute percentage error.

of the three types of assets, based on their rates of return, and then normalizing the weights into shares. For each type of asset, I, an equation of the form

$$\text{WEIGHT}(\text{I}) = a(\text{I}) + b(\text{I}) * \text{RETURN}(\text{I}) + c(\text{I}) * \text{CHGRET}(\text{I}) \qquad \textbf{(4.42–44)}$$
$$+ \; d(\text{I}) * \text{TIME}$$

is evaluated. CHGRET is the ratio of the current rate of return to a moving average of past rates of return, a proxy for the expected capital gain. The parameters of equations 4.42–44 (see table 4.2) were estimated from national flow-of-funds data, using shares as the left-hand variable.[28]

Chapter 5. The Households

The people who populate the households in our model come in two sexes and four occupations. At all times, they know their current situation: whether they are employed, by whom and at what wage, whether they have a spouse and whether the spouse is working, what the value and character of their assets and debts are, what the age of their car is. They also have access to knowledge about the economy, such as the rate of inflation and the rate of unemployment. Many elements of a household's situation at any moment in time are the result of actions taken previously. The household may have a debt secured by a mortgage on a house or obligations to a bank as a result of purchases in previous periods. The value of assets reflects past saving decisions, and the current composition of the portfolio results from past decisions concerning which assets to acquire.

In addition to knowledge about their situation, people in the model have a repertoire of decisionmaking processes and activities, which they follow in each round of the action. As workers, they seek, continue in, or leave employment; as members of consuming households, they spend for consumption, pay taxes, make installment payments on past debt, contract new debt, and adjust the composition of their asset portfolios. All of the households have the same tastes in consumer goods; all of them make purchases of goods and services from firms according to the same linear expenditure system, after paying taxes to the governments and debt service to the bank and the financial intermediary.

Differences in each persons' situation and history result in differences in their actions. For example, a person in the managerial and professional occupational group earns a relatively high salary, experiences little unemployment, has probably accumulated an asset portfolio of above average size, and consumes accordingly.

For a simulation starting at the beginning of 1972, a labor force of size

675 and a retired population of 100 are represented in an array in the computer memory. The labor-force size changes appropriately during the period, and the number of retired persons changes as labor force members exit the labor force (see chapter 2 for discussion of the scale). Other persons (young children, for example) who would have zero probability of entering the labor force in the time period being simulated do not appear in the array, and the only economic activity they are represented as engaging in is the consumption of goods and services. For some of them, this consumption is financed through expenditures made on their behalf by workers or retired persons. The remainder—the welfare population—receive government transfer payments, which it devotes entirely to consumption expenditures. The receipt of transfers and consumption expenditures by the welfare group are dealt with aggregatively.[1]

For those persons explicitly represented, the major items of information that are kept current in the course of a run are shown in table 5.1.

Personal Characteristics

The first five items in table 5.1 contain information on personal characteristics that affect economic participation. Storing in memory the identity, if any, of the person's spouse, ISPOUS, allows two persons represented in the array of actual or potential labor force participants to keep house together, in the sense of having joint decisionmaking on consumption and saving and having consolidated debts, assets, and ownership of home and automobiles.

Each worker is attached to one of four broad occupational groups: (1) managers, administrators, professionals, and technical workers; (2) clerks and sales persons; (3) craft workers and operatives; and (4) service workers and laborers (see table 2.1 for characteristics). Employers hire an inexperienced labor-force entrant into any occupational group, within exogenously imposed sex quotas. Experienced workers, however, are usually considered only for job openings in the occupational group in which they have experience. However, if there is a shortage in any occupation, employers relax this constraint.

The variable IDIS is used as a measure of the individual's place in the distribution of persons within his or her occupational group with respect to productivity, and is a proxy for education and other forms of human capital.[2] ISTIG is set equal to one for those persons who have a greater than average difficulty in finding a job when they are unemployed. This variable (whose distribution in the population can be varied) was created to take account of the great disparity in duration of unemployment and to add realism to evaluations of policies designed to help the unemployed. It is a crude proxy for age and race (Bergmann 1974a).

Table 5.1. Information available concerning each fictional household

Personal characteristics

ISEX	Sex.
ISPOUS	Identity of spouse (0 if unmarried; −1 if married but spouse not in array; address of spouse if latter is in array).
IOWN	1 if homeowner; 0, otherwise.
OWNCAR	1 if possible car owner; 0, otherwise.
HTASTE(I,NOH)	Value governing taste for ıth asset of household NOH.

Labor force status

LF	1 if in labor force; 0, otherwise.
ICASTE	Occupation 1–4 of present or last job; 5 if new to labor force.
IDIS	Skill level within occupation: −1, 0, +1.
ISTIG	1 if at a disadvantage in being hired when unemployed; 0, otherwise.
IRETIR	1 if once represented in labor force; 0, otherwise.
IEMPST	Employer identity, if employed; 0, otherwise.
IUDAT	Date of last accession to or separation from employment.
IELIGW	Unemployment insurance eligibility, in weeks.
UI	1 if currently receiving unemployment insurance; 0, otherwise.

Financial status

HASSET(I,NOH)	Current holdings by household NOH of ıth asset: 1, cash; 2, savings accounts; 3, treasury bills; 4, treasury bonds; 5, municipal bonds; 6, private bonds; 7, real estate; 8, equities.
HLIAB(I,NOH)	Current liability of ıth type of household NOH: 1, current noninstallment consumer debt; 2, current payoff value of mortgage indebtedness.
AMORT	Payment due on installment loan in each round.
ISTART	Date of last automobile purchase and initial installment payment.
AMORTG	Payment due on home mortgage in each round.
INMORT	Starting date of mortgage (0 for home renters).

Labor-Force Status

At the beginning of a run, some of the persons represented in the COMMON block are marked off as being in the labor force (LF = 1), and a proportion of them equal to the actual U.S. employment rate is marked off as being employed. Those employed are attached to particular firms in accordance with the distribution of employees by industry in the U.S. GNP accounts. Thereafter, the size of the labor force, XLABF, is controlled by a set of macroeconomic equations:

$$\text{LFMALE} = a(1) + a(2)*\text{TPOPM} + a(3)*\text{SAVURA}(24) \qquad (5.1)$$
$$+ \; a(4)*\text{TIME};$$

$$\text{LFFEMA} = a(1) + a(2)*\text{TPOPF} + a(3)*\text{SAVURA}(12) \qquad (5.2)$$
$$+ \; a(4)*\text{TIME};$$

$$\text{XLABF} = (\text{LFMALE} + \text{LFFEMA}) * \text{SCALE}, \qquad (5.3)$$

where TPOPM and TPOPF are the male and female population, respectively, of the United States; SAVURA(12) is the unemployment rate lagged six months; TIME is the number of the current round (1967 = 1); LFMALE is the male labor force and LFFEMA is the female labor force. Equations 5.1 and 5.2, which are estimated from monthly data for the period 1967–79, are fitted to U.S. macrodata. The sum in equation 5.3 is scaled to model size. When equation 5.3 calls for a net shrinkage of the labor force, unemployed persons are chosen at random to leave; when net growth of the labor force occurs, nonparticipants are chosen to enter the labor force as unemployed persons and to search for jobs. The relative size of each sex group is kept in line with U.S. data by choosing persons of the appropriate sex to enter and of the appropriate sex and occupation to leave.

As the simulation proceeds, persons enter the ranks of the unemployed by entering the labor force, being laid off, or quitting. The quit rate per round is controlled by

$$\text{QUITR} = a(1) + a(2){*}\text{URATE}, \tag{5.4}$$

with employed persons being chosen at random to quit (Schultze 1976).

The process by which employers choose the number of workers in each occupational group to lay off or hire is described in chapter 4. When layoffs are required, persons to be laid off are chosen at random from among those the firm employs. (Layoffs of those with least seniority could be programmed, at the cost of some slowing in the run time.) When a firm needs to hire, candidates are selected at random from the ranks of the unemployed to come to an interview. Unless the worker refuses a job offer or the employer refuses to take the worker, a hire takes place.

The probability that a worker refuses an offered job is assigned different values in different circumstances. The higher this probability, the tighter the labor market is for a given unemployment rate and the greater the delay is in filling a job vacancy, since a maximum number of interviews per round per job is specified. On the basis of evidence that few unemployed workers refuse job offers (Lerner 1981; Sheppard and Belitsky 1966), we set the probability of a worker refusal at .1 for the runs reported here—unless he or she is receiving unemployment insurance, in which case the probability is set at .2. The probability that an employer will refuse a worker has been set at zero, unless that worker is stigmatized as hard to hire. In this case, the worker is turned down by employers with a probability of .5. Except in tight labor markets, these probabilities of refusal do not affect the unemployment rate. They do, however, affect the distribution of durations of spells of unemployment (Bergmann 1974b).

Every time a worker leaves a job or enters a job, note is made of the date of the event, which is stored in IUDAT. A newly unemployed worker's record of entitlement of unemployment insurance (stored in IELIGW) is adjusted upward to twenty-four rounds (twenty-six calendar weeks) if he or she has been in covered employment continuously for twenty-four rounds.

Income

Wage Income

Each employed worker is paid a wage each round:

$$\text{WAGE} = \text{WAGEF(ICASTE,IFIRM)}*[1 + a(1)*\text{IDIS}], \tag{5.5}$$

which is dependent on the average wage the employer is currently paying to workers of that occupation in the worker's position in the skill-level distribution of workers of that occupation, IDIS.[3]

Unemployment Insurance

Those workers who are unemployed and who have entitlement to unemployment insurance are paid at a benefit level that depends on their previous wage and time:

$$\text{BEN} = a(1) + a(2)*\text{WAGE} + a(3)*\text{TIME}. \tag{5.6}$$

Those excluded from unemployment insurance include those who started their period of unemployment by entering or reentering the labor force, those who have exhausted their eligibility, and those who have worked in uncovered employment, a proportion that dwindles through time. Unemployment insurance payments are exempt from social insurance and income taxes.

Nonlabor Income

Individuals who have at one time been, but no longer are, in the labor force next receive nontaxable transfers from the federal and state/local governments in uniform, exogenously determined amounts.

At this point, households are paid interest and dividends on assets owned. Assets of two workers who are married to each other are consolidated, as are their income-tax computations and payments and spending decisions. Interest is received on savings deposits, HASSET(2,NOH), at a rate set for the current round by the bank (see chapter 6). Next, interest is paid on household holdings of fixed-interest securities—treasury bills, HASSET(3,NOH); treasury bonds, HASSET(4,NOH); municipal bonds, HASSET(5,NOH); and private bonds, HASSET(6,NOH)—at the original interest rate for the security. Finally, dividends are paid on equities, HASSET(8,NOH), at rates that fluctuate with profits of the firms (see chapter 4). The interest and dividends on open-market securities are paid to households by the financial intermediary, which collects interest and dividend payments from the original issuers of the securities.

Fixed Outlays

Social-Insurance Taxes

Each employed worker pays social insurance, SSTAX, to the federal government of

$$\text{SSTAX} = \text{POL}(9)*MIN[\text{WAGE},\text{POL}(7)], \tag{5.7}$$

where POL(9) and POL(7) are the social-insurance tax rate and the maximum tax base, respectively, set annually by the federal government.[4]

Principal and Interest on Outstanding Debt

Each household's next order of business is to make interest and amortization payments on outstanding debts incurred previously. Debts arise from loans for automobiles, retail spending, and mortgages. As amorization payments are made, the recorded size of each form of debt goes down.

Automobile Debt. This kind of debt arises when a consumer buys a car; for convenience, these loans are originally made by the bank, which sets the current interest rate on them, but some of them are sold by the bank to the financial intermediary and the trade firm. These loans are paid off in NPAY installments of equal size, with NPAY being set arbitrarily at 144, or three years. The date of the loan, ISTART, is remembered, and the loan is paid off at date ISTART + NPAY. The size of the installment due each round, AMORT, is computed at the time the debt is incurred:

$$\overline{\text{AMORT}} = \text{AMT}*\text{RNEW}*(1 + \text{RNEW})**\text{NPAY}/ \tag{5.8}$$
$$[(1 + \text{RNEW})**\text{NPAY} - 1],$$

where AMT is the amount of the loan and RNEW is the current interest rate per round on consumer loans.

When a consumer who already has an installment loan needs a new one because of subsequent purchases or because of inability to pay an installment, the bank takes account of the size and number of payments scheduled on the old loan, discounts them at the original consumer interest rate to obtain the unpaid capital amount of the old obligation, and consolidates the old and new loans, resulting in new values for AMORT and ISTART and a new schedule of NPAY.

Retail-Credit Liabilities. These debts, HLIAB(1,NOH), primarily arise from retail revolving-credit accounts. The bank administers their origin and servicing but sells a portion to the financial intermediary and the trade firm. The household makes interest payments each round at the current per-round interest rate for consumer debt, RNEW, on the amount outstanding and amortizes 1/NPAY of that amount.

Mortgage Loan Liabilities.   Loans secured by mortgages arise on the occasion of a household's first purchase of a house or on the occasion of shifting from one house to another of a different size. New or enlarged mortgages are granted by the financial intermediary, which also sets current rates for new mortgages. The ownership of existing mortgages is shared among the federal government, the bank, and the financial intermediary, although the last named collects interest and amortization payments on behalf of the others. All mortgages run for 1,200 rounds (twenty-five years). The size of the amortization payment due in each round, AMORTG, is set on the occasion of the issuance of the mortgage, which takes place when a new home is purchased (discussed below). It depends on the value of the house, HVALUE, the down payment, DOWN, and the current interest rate for new mortgages, RMC:

$$\text{AMORTG} = [\text{HVALUE} - \text{DOWN}] \tag{5.9}$$
$$*\{[\text{RMC}*(1 + \text{RMC})**1200]/[1 + \text{RMC}**1199]\}.$$

For each household with mortgage debt, three pieces of information are remembered: INMORT, the month in which the mortgage was taken out; AMORTG, the payment incorporating interest and amortization, which must be paid each round; and HLIAB(2,NOH), the current principal owing. This enables us to separate debt service into payment of interest and repayment of principal for purposes of tax liabilities and national accounting.

Real-Estate Taxes and Home-Repair Costs

The financial intermediary pays to the state/local government all property taxes owed by homeowners, and to the construction firm all expenses for repair of their homes. Homeowners pay TAXREP to the financial intermediary for these items in proportion to the current value of their homes, HASSET(7,NOH):[5]

$$\text{TAXREP} = \text{ESCROW}*\text{HASSET}(7,\text{NOH})/ \sum_{\text{NOH}} \text{HASSET}(7,\text{NOH}), \tag{5.10}$$

where ESCROW is the historic flow for these items in the national income and product accounts.

Personal Income Taxes

Households have now made all of the contractual payments that affect their income-tax liabilities and have received all taxable income. Federal income taxes are computed on YTBLE, which is the sum of wages, property income, government transfer payments subject to taxation, and negative or positive taxable-income carryovers from previous rounds. Seven policy variables control taxes paid: the exempted income per person, POL(1); the minimum tax rate, POL(2); the rate at which average tax rates for married persons increase with taxable income, POL(3); the percentage of income allowed as deduction, POL(4); the maximum deduction if not itemizing deductions, POL(5); the ratio of state/local income taxes to federal income taxes, POL(6); and the maximum tax rate, POL(17). Rates are adjusted for marital status by setting ISPOU equal to zero for unmarried persons and equal to one for married persons:[6]

$$\text{DEDUCT} = (3.5**\text{ISPOU})*\text{POL}(1) + MAX\{\text{PYINT} + \text{AMORTG} - \text{PAYCAP} \\ + \text{TAXREP}, MIN[\text{POL}(4)*\text{YTBLE}, \text{POL}(5)]\}. \quad \textbf{(5.11)}$$

If YNET = YTBLE − DEDUCT is negative, the household has no income-tax liability in the current round, and the negative amount is cumulated in TFUND(NOH) and deducted from YTBLE in future rounds. If YNET is positive, the federal tax owed is

$$\text{TAX} = [\text{POL}(2)*\text{YNET} + \text{POL}(3)*\text{YNET}**2]*.77**\text{ISPOUS}. \quad \textbf{(5.12)}$$

For high-income families, the formula is altered to take account of the maximum tax rate.

State/local income taxes are computed as proportional to federal income taxes:

$$\text{SLYTAX} = \text{POL}(6)*\text{TAX}. \quad \textbf{(5.13)}$$

The value of POL(6) is the annually determined historic ratio of state/local income taxes to federal income taxes.

Residential Rent

Renters pay to the real-estate industry[7]

$$\text{RENT} = (1 + \text{ISPOU}))*\text{P(IREAL)}*a(1) + a(2)*\text{YATC}, \quad \textbf{(5.14)}$$

where YATC is income left after income taxes and payments to creditors. After these payments are made, both renters and owners have paid all housing expenses.

Further Spending and Saving Decisions

Increasing Retail-Credit Liability

Households wish to borrow DLOAN a fixed fraction of their last-round retail spending EXP(NOH)$_o$. They add DLOAN to their retail-credit liabilities:

$$\text{DLOAN} = a(1)*\text{EXP(NOH)}_o. \quad \textbf{(5.15)}$$

They now compute the funds available for spending on items other than housing and automobiles, after taking account of obligatory payments for taxes and debt service. For a household that has recently suffered a drop in income, spending will be greater than the remainder of spendable income, with the excess spending financed either through a drawdown of assets or through a loan.

Cash flow considered available for spending is

wages + transfers + property income + DLOAN + CAPGAN,

where DLOAN is the increase in new noninstallment debt decided upon, and CAPGAN is 0.5 percent of the change in market value of the household's marketable securities.[8] Obligatory payments are

social security taxes + income taxes + housing expenditures +
AMORTG + REPAY + PYINT,

in which AMORTG, REPAY, and PYINT are debt-service items. At this point, the household has made all of these obligatory payments, leaving the remainder of spendable cash flow

$$\text{YDIS} = \text{cash flow} - \text{obligatory payments}, \tag{5.16}$$

which controls the remainder of desired spending for goods and services other than housing and automobiles.

Each household next computes the current cost of buying the minimum physical amounts of each firm's product that it wishes to consume each period, regardless of price. This bundle can be thought of as the household's subsistence requirement for these goods, and its cost is

$$\text{SUBSIS} = \sum_{\text{IFIRM}} a(\text{IFIRM})*\text{P}(\text{IFIRM})*[1 + \text{CTRADE}(\text{IFIRM})] \tag{5.17}$$

$$*2**\text{ISPOU},$$

where P(IFIRM) is the current price of a unit of firm IFIRM's output, and the coefficients a(IFIRM) give physical quantities (see equation 5.19 and table 5.1). The CTRADE(IFIRM) are trade margins paid by retail consumers to the trade industry and are based on the 1972 input/output coefficients. ISPOU is zero for single persons and one for married couples.

The determination of total spending for goods and services other than housing and autos, EXP(NOH), occurs next. It is one of the major saving decisions of the household. (The others are the various decisions as to changes in outstanding consumer debts.) We assume three goals for the household: (1) It desires to purchase at least the subsistence requirements, SUBSIS. (2) It desires to adjust expenditures only slowly from their previous value, EXP(NOH)_o.[9] (3) If EXP has not changed, it desires to add to assets a fixed proportion of the amount by which YDIS exceeds subsistence requirements:

$$\text{EXP(NOH)} = a(1)*\text{EXP(NOH)}_o \qquad (5.18)$$
$$+ [1 - a(1)]*[\text{SUBSIS} + a(2)*MAX(\text{YDIS} - \text{SUBSIS}),0].$$

Retail Purchases

Having decided on the level of total purchases of goods and services other than housing and automobiles, EXP(NOH), the household now distributes that amount of spending among the remaining firms according to a Stone/Geary linear expenditures system.[10] From each firm, the household buys a physical quantity:

$$\text{BUY} = a(\text{IFIRM}) + b(\text{IFIRM})* \left[\frac{\text{EXP(NOH)} - \text{SUBSIS}}{\text{P(IFIRM)}} \right], \qquad (5.19)$$

for which P(IFIRM)*BUY is paid to IFIRM. An amount equal to BUY* CTRADE(IFIRM) is paid by the household to the trade firm as a retail markup on the purchase. Table 5.2 gives the values of the consumption parameters $a(\text{IFIRM})$, $b(\text{IFIRM})$. and CTRADE(IFIRM).[11]

Purchase of a Home

Households that currently rent dwelling units but are potential homeowners next consider whether to try to buy a home, and current homeowners decide whether to purchase a different home. Renters try to purchase a home only if

Table 5.2. Household consumption parameters

IFIRM	$a(\text{IFIRM})$	$b(\text{IFIRM})$	CTRADE(IFIRM)
Agriculture	0.00	0.024	0.524
Mining	0.03	0.000	0.984
Other durable manufacturing	0.00	0.150	0.748
Nondurable manufacturing	10.23	0.375	0.650
Capital-intensive service	0.68	0.124	0.000
Other service	16.46	0.078	0.002
Real estate	2.71	0.210	0.000
Financial intermediary	2.96	0.006	0.001
Bank	0.40	0.004	0.002
Federal government enterprises	0.00	0.009	0.000
State/local government enterprises	0.00	0.001	0.004
Rest-of-world	0.01	0.019	0.008

NOTE: For treatment of home and automotive purchases and payments, see text.

all household members in the labor force are employed and the household has a cushion of discretionary income, so that EXP(NOH) $\geq$ SUBSIS. Then they take into account the price of the services for a round of a rental housing unit, P(RENT), the purchase price of an equivalent housing unit, P(OWN), and the mortgage interest rate R(7) on that capital sum. The proportion of renters wanting to shift to owning is

$$\text{PSHIFT} = a(1)*\text{P(RENT)}/[\text{P(OWN)}*\text{R(7)}]. \tag{5.20}$$

The appropriate number of households are then chosen at random as potential home buyers from among eligible renters. A household is able to buy a home only if it currently has assets to cover the down payment and closing costs (whose determination is described below) and if a house and the mortgage money to finance its purchase are available.[12]

Customers for houses are taken care of in the order in which they appear in the array of households. Professional and managerial households appear at the beginning of the array, so they get the first crack at new homes on the market.

Renters decide how much they are willing to pay for the new home by relating the monthly cost of owning a house to the rent they are currently paying:

$$\text{AMORTG} + \text{TAXREP} = a(1)*\text{RENT}. \tag{5.21}$$

The value of the house to be purchased, HVALUE, is then obtained by solving equation (5.9). The ratio of PDOWN to HVALUE is assumed to be set exogenously by POL(18). HVALUE varies directly with the household's income and inversely with the mortgage interest rate. The physical characteristics of the house that can be purchased currently for HVALUE (or the number of physical units included in it, in our model's terms) depends on P(OWN), the price per unit of owned homes.

The purchase of the new home will proceed if the household has sufficient liquid assets to pay the down payment and closing costs (CLOSE, which is 5 percent of HVALUE). The house is purchased if

$$\text{HASSET(1,NOH)} + \text{HASSET(2,NOH)} + \text{HASSET(3,NOH)} \tag{5.22}$$
$$> (\text{PDOWN} + \text{CLOSE})*\text{HVALUE},$$

in which the items on the left are the household's cash, savings accounts, and short-term marketable securities, respectively. If this test is not met, the household waits to purchase a new home until more saving has occurred.

Delivery of the house is noted by reducing TRUST, the inventory of completed but unsold homes managed by the financial intermediary, and by recording the value of the house among the household's assets. When TRUST is down to zero, the remainder of households wanting to purchase homes must put off their purchases.

Homeowners' calculations to upgrade are similar to those of renters when the latter decide to switch to owning. They first calculate a shadow value for rent by using equation (5.14). This gives the currently desired value of AMORTG by using equation (5.21) and the value of HVALUE by using equation (5.9). If the number of physical units that currently can be purchased for this amount is greater than the number of units the family now owns (assuming currently desired AMORTG is greater than the actual AMORTG), then the old house is turned in to the real-estate firm and a new house is purchased. The old mortgage is cancelled and a new one, at current interest rates, is negotiated, for the difference between the value of the new house and the household's equity in the old house. In the model, 0.5 percent of homeowners consider buying a new home each round.

Purchase of an Automobile

Households that own cars are arbitrarily designated as *always* owning cars, while the rest never do. A car-owning household purchases a new automobile, provided that (1) no member of the household in the labor force is unemployed, (2) previous automobile installment debts have been repaid fully, and (3) there are enough assets to meet the down payment. The household decides on the size of the real increment in desired automobile ownership by a process similar to the decision process for home purchase.

A down payment of 20 percent of the purchase price is required; thus, a monthly payment on any new auto purchase of BUYCAR physical units is

$$\text{DMORT} = (.8*\text{BUYCAR}*\text{PAUTO})*\frac{\text{RNEW}*(1 + \text{RENEW})^{\text{NPAY}}}{(1 + \text{RNEW})^{\text{NPAY}-1}}, \quad (5.23)$$

where PAUTO is the current price of a physical unit of automobiles, and RNEW is the interest rate on auto loans.[13]

The desired value of DMORT is taken to be

$$\text{DMORT} = a(1)*\text{EXP}(\text{NOH}), \quad (5.24)$$

where EXP is, as above, the moving average of the household's expenditures for goods and services other than housing and automobiles.[14] The household's weekly installment payments, AMORT(NOH), are set at DMORT; the date, ISTART, is recorded, and the appropriate funds for the transactions are transferred. If the automobile manufacturing firm does not currently possess sufficient inventory of automobiles to fill the household's order, the order is backlogged and filled in the next round of activity.

Adjusting the Portfolio

For accounting purposes, the household values all assets, except its real estate and equities, at cost; real estate and equities are valued at current market price, appropriately depreciated in the case of real estate. The various receipts and payments of the current round have affected the value of the household's total assets, HASSET(9,NOH), which is now updated to

$$
\begin{aligned}
\text{HASSET}(9,\text{NOH}) = \ & \text{HASSET}(9,\text{NOH})_o \\
& + [\text{YDIS} - \text{CAPGAN} - \text{EXP}(\text{NOH})] \\
& + [\text{CHPREQ}*\text{HASSET}(8,\text{NOH})/\text{TOTASS}(8)] \\
& + [\text{HASSET}(7,\text{NOH}) - \text{HASSET}(7,\text{NOH})_o] \\
& + [\text{EQUI} - \text{DOWN} - \text{CLOSE} - \text{DOWNP}],
\end{aligned}
\tag{5.25}
$$

in which the first bracketed quantity is current-account cash receipts, YDIS − CAPGAN, less expenditures; the second bracketed quantity is the change in market value of the household's equities; the third bracketed quantity is the change in the value of the household's real estate; and the fourth bracketed quantity is the net cash flow from current purchases of homes and automobiles.

Next the household computes the share of its assets it wishes to keep in cash, savings accounts, treasury bills, treasury bonds, municipal bonds, private bonds, and equities. It computes weights for each asset, depending on the size of the household's portfolio, the current rate of return, and expected change in the rate of return on the asset in question:

$$
\begin{aligned}
\text{WEIGHT}(\text{I},\text{J}) = \ & a(\text{I}) + b(\text{I})*\text{RETURN}(\text{I}) + c(\text{I})*\text{ASSETS}(\text{J}) \\
& + d(\text{I})*\text{CHGRET}(\text{I}) + e(\text{I})*\text{TIME}.
\end{aligned}
\tag{5.26}
$$

RETURN(I) is the current interest or dividend return, if any, on the asset in question. An indicator of expected capital gain or loss from expected changes in interest or dividend rates, CHGRET is zero for the first three assets; for the others, it is the ratio of its current interest or dividend rate to a moving average of its past rates. Values of the parameters of these equations are given in table 5.3.

Table 5.3. Parameters of household demand for financial assets

Asset	a	b	c	d	e	AAPE[a]	$\bar{R}^2$
Cash	0.0727		−0.3107		0.000037	2.61	.84
	(88.03)		(−1.92)		(16.6)		
Savings accounts	0.1794	0.8704	−0.5713		0.000344	3.35	.96
	(3.33)	(0.77)	(−1.53)		(8.06)		
Treasury bills	−0.00017	0.2370	0.00516		−0.000009	29.10	.58
	(−0.075)	(6.00)	(0.49)		(−2.27)		
Bonds	0.1403	0.7997	0.1139	−0.0608	0.000022	3.09	.81
	(11.80)	(2.32)	(0.49)	(−2.79)	(1.40)		
Equities	0.5802		0.7629	0.00505	−0.00049	2.78	.97
	(19.75)		(2.86)	(1.85)	(−44.46)		

NOTE: t-statistics are in parentheses. The $c(\text{I})$ were estimated from the 1972 Consumer Expenditure Survey.

[a]Average absolute percentage error.

Table 5.4. Household portfolio distribution, by size, mid-1972 (percentage)

	Portfolio Size		
Asset	Small ($100)	Average ($12,662)	Large ($100,000)
Cash	9.5	8.4	0.0
Savings accounts	34.4	32.2	4.7
Treasury bills	0.0	1.0	41.6
Bonds	15.6	12.9	0.0
Equities	40.5	45.5	53.7

At the end of each round, the current period's weights are used by each household to adjust the quantities of each asset in its portfolio. If an asset has negative weight, the household is assumed to have zero demand for that asset. Other weights are normalized to shares. Assets are bought and sold (through the financial intermediary) to bring them into line with desired amounts. Table 5.4 presents the percentage distribution of the assets in three sample portfolios in mid-1972 determined by the parameters in table 5.3.

Chapter 6. The Financial Institutions

In this chapter we describe how the money markets operate in the Transactions Model: how the buying, selling, and holding of financial claims is represented and how the financial institutions set interest rates. The operations of the monetary authority, which sets the policy framework within which the financial institutions operate, are discussed in the next chapter.

The private financial sector consists of the bank and the financial intermediary. Paradoxically, the most important money-market activities we have programmed for the financial institutions, such as making loans and buying and selling securities on their own and others' account, do not enter into the product side of the national income accounts. What does count there as their product is a melange of service items, some of which are paid for directly by households and firms (such as brokerage commissions and trustees' fees) and some of which are imputed services, delivered without direct payment but balanced off by profits on lending (free checking services, for example; see table 6.1). The financial institutions are profit-making and engage in all activities discussed for firms in chapter 4, such as interindustry sales and purchases, hiring, wage setting, paying dividends, and so on.[1] In addition to setting interest rates, financial institutions set the prices they charge for their nonlending services.

Financial-Market Activities

The two financial institutions whose activities are individually described in detail below have as their *raison d'etre* the marketing of all the debt the other actors incur and the creation of financial instruments. These financial instruments include demand deposits, bank loans, the firms' bonds and equities, the governments' bonds, and mortgages.

71

Table 6.1. Outputs of financial firms in the national income and product accounts

Firm	Type of Service	Form of Transaction
Bank	Banking services, paid for by service charges	Cash
	Trust services	Cash
	Services of the monetary authority corresponding to net income	Imputed
	Services corresponding in value to net income of banks	Imputed
Financial intermediary	Brokerage services	Cash
	Insurance services (insurance premiums less payments and customers' equity buildup)	Imputed

The bank operates checking accounts for all the firms, households, and governments, and creates bank loans for them according to rules described in previous chapters. It also decides on the current interest rate for bank loans and influences the size of its portfolio through discounting and debt flotation. It allocates its portfolio of assets among bank loans and other assets. The bank must take into account constraints laid on it by the monetary authority.

The financial intermediary makes the market in debt instruments other than bank loans and holds some of each instrument for its own account. In its market-making function, it sets current yields of each instrument. It may borrow heavily from the bank to finance its holdings.

The financing of home mortgages engages three actors—the bank, the financial intermediary, and the federal government. (In actuality, money for home mortgages in the United States comes largely from savings and loan associations, federal government agencies that purchase mortgages from the savings and loans, banks, and insurance companies.) In the model, total savings deposits are determined endogenously by households. The share held in savings and loan associations (SLs) is exogenous, as is the share of household deposits that the SLs invest in mortgages.[2] The government agencies' behavior is taken to be exogenous. The amounts of mortgages that banks and insurance companies hold are determined by their portfolio-allocation process, described below.

As described in chapter 4, the real-estate firm needs a projection thirty rounds ahead of new mortgages the financial institutions are committed to purchase. This projection is done by applying the rate of change between two moving averages of net acquisition, whose average lags differ by thirty rounds.

The Bank

Assets and Liabilities

The bank represents the activities of all commercial banks and savings institutions in the flow-of-funds accounts. All of the actors, with the exception of the monetary authority and the bank itself, keep money in the form of demand deposits, which are liabilities of the bank. No currency is represented. When transactions occur, demand deposits are transferred from the account of one actor to that of another through the operation of the TRANS subroutine (see chapter 2).

Money in the form of demand deposits is created whenever the bank makes a payment to an economic agent other than the monetary authority; that is, when the bank grants a bank loan, purchases securities in the open market, or pays wages, rents, or dividends. Money is destroyed whenever an economic agent other than the monetary authority makes a payment to the bank. Savings accounts at the bank are created or destroyed in the amounts desired by households, as explained in chapter 5.

The bank has a portfolio of financial assets consisting of (1) bank loan instruments, whose genesis is described in chapters 4 and 5 and whose supply limitations are described below; (2) mortgages, whose acquisitions are determined as explained below; (3) consumer credit, consisting of an exogenously determined share of total consumer credit outstanding; (4) treasury bills, which are three-month securities issued by the federal government; (5) bonds of the federal and state/local governments and of the firms; and (6) a reserve account at the monetary authority, whose size is controlled by open-market operations of the latter and by the discounting activity of the bank.

The bank's liabilities consist of (1) demand and savings deposits; (2) discounts at the monetary authority with a maturity of one week; and (3) other debt and equity instruments issued by the bank, such as bonds, stocks, and large-denomination certificates of deposit, all consolidated under a vector BONDS(IBANK,IMAT), where the instruments have maturities IMAT of up to twelve months into the future.

The desired ratio, DEBTR, of the bank's own debt outstanding to its financial assets is determined by:[3]

$$\text{DEBTR} = a(1) + a(2)*\text{RBON} - \text{RBILL}) + a(3)*\text{TIME}, \qquad (6.1)$$

where RBON and RBILL are the current interest rates on bonds and bills, respectively. The bank issues or retires sufficient bonds to bring the sum of the indebtedness to the desired amount.

Loans

In the course of a run, the bank is approached by households, nonfinancial firms, and the financial intermediary for new loans. The bank's customers are programmed to make payments of interest and principal on their outstanding bank loans on schedule, and the schedule is revised when loans are made or extinguished.

Nonfinancial firms take out bank loans repayable in one lump sum twelve rounds (one quarter) later. The loans occur when these firms must finance purchases, wages, or dividends and lack the funds to do so. They also occur when firms wish to increase their stock of liquid assets. The financial intermediary is allowed an essentially unlimited line of credit in order that it may play its role of making a market in open-market securities.

Households have access to car loans and mortgage credit from the bank on certain set occasions if they meet income and job-holding requirements and have the assets for down payments (see Chapter 5). These loans are repaid in even payments each round. In addition, households apply for loans sufficient to maintain credit-card debits proportional to the income they have left over after taxes and debt amortization. Bank loans to households are amortized when households wish to reduce their indebtedness; interest is paid each round on the outstanding balance.

The rules of thumb the bank's customers are programmed to follow when deciding on the stock of loans they wish to have outstanding derive from the limits to borrowing permitted by the bank and the prudential limits customers place on themselves. We have not distinguished the supply-side constraints from the demand-side constraints.

The bank influences the amount of bank loans demanded by the other actors through its setting of the interest rates for its business and consumer loans, RBLO and RCONS, respectively. (The generation of the demand for bank loans by firms and households is described in chapters 4 and 5.) Setting interest rates is dealt with in detail below; loan rates are raised when the value of loans in the bank's portfolio is greater than considered optimal under its own rules of thumb, which may occur when the bank is short of reserves. Rates are lowered in the opposite case.

Consumer-credit instruments are held as assets by the bank, as well as by the financial intermediary and the trade firm. The distribution of total consumer-credit assets by holder is done exogenously by reference to the flow-of-funds accounts.

Reserves

Against its deposit liabilities, the bank is required to hold reserves, RESREQ, in the form of a deposit at the monetary authority:

$$\text{RESREQ} = \text{POL}(21)*\text{TCASH} + \text{POL}(22)*\text{TOTSAC}, \qquad (6.2)$$

where POL(21) and POL(22) are reserve ratios set by the monetary authority as part of its policy implementation. TCASH is all demand deposits except those owned by the bank itself, and TOTSAC is the sum of all of the households' savings deposits.

The bank's actual reserves, RESERV, are held in the form of a deposit at the monetary authority. Reserves are created whenever the monetary authority makes a payment, which occurs only through open-market purchases and discounting. Reserves are destroyed whenever a payment is made to the monetary authority, which occurs only through open-market sales and repayment of discounts. Only through discounting can the bank through its own actions change the quantity of its reserves. This conforms relatively closely with the conditions of the banking system in the United States but not with the options open to an individual bank, which can engage in transactions that will transfer reserves from or to other banks.

Toward the end of each round, after all of its customers for bank loans, mortgages, and consumer credit have been dealt with, and after the monetary authority has conducted open-market operations, the bank reviews its reserve situation. The granting of new loans, the interest payments received, the repayments of the principal on loans, and increases and decreases in savings deposits affect the amount of reserves required. The quantity of reserves has been affected by the open-market operations of the monetary authority since the bank's last review of the reserve situation in the previous round and by repayment of discounts by the bank.

The process controlling the generation of new loans for the bank's customers may permit a rise in bank loans during the round sufficient to cause required reserves to rise above actual reserves. The rationale we use is that bank loans are the bank's most lucrative investment, and it is willing to meet a surge in demand for them in part by discounting and in part by disposing of other assets.

If the bank's end-of-round review discloses a reserve deficiency, it moves toward meeting the deficiency by (1) discounting at the monetary authority and (2) selling open-market securities from its portfolio to the financial intermediary for cash, which extinguishes demand deposits.

Current practices in the United States mandate that actual reserves averaged over a one-week period must be at least equal to required reserves based on deposits two weeks earlier. The Federal Reserve accommodates a reserve-deficient banking system by making temporary purchases (under repurchase agreements) of government bills from the banking system on one day and selling them back to the banks on the following day. Despite this safety valve, which has the practical effect of softening the reserve requirement, banks with deficient reserves are under considerable pressure from the Federal Reserve to move toward an equality of required and actual reserves.

We attempt to reflect this situation in the model by allowing the bank to employ the two steps above to meet reserve requirements but allowing it to stop short of achieving equality of actual and required reserves. The bank first decides what part, if any, of the deficiency will be met by discounting at the monetary authority. Discounting depends on the current treasury-bill rate, the ratio of excess to required reserves, and time:

$$\text{DISCNT} = a(1) + a(2)*\text{RBIL} + a(3)*(\text{EXRES} / \text{RESREQ}) \qquad (6.3)$$
$$+ a(4)*\text{TIME},$$

in which RBIL is the current bill rate, EXRES is excess reserves, RESREQ is required reserves, and TIME is time, with the first round of 1967 equal to one. The reserve deficiency remaining after this discounting is taken care of partially by sales of open-market securities by the bank to the financial intermediary for cash. This action extinguishes demand deposits and reduces required reserves to the extent that the financial intermediary can acquire the securities by paying for them out of its current stock of cash. A cash deficiency on the part of the financial intermediary at this point is made up by borrowing from the bank, but this transaction does not affect the bank's reserve position until the following round.[4]

We have traced in detail the response of the bank to a reserve deficiency. If, in contrast, the end-of-round review reveals a reserve excess, the bank purchases open-market securities equal to a fraction of the undesired reserve excess. A slack demand for loans produces these periods of excess reserves.

Interest rates for bank loans are changed by the bank if the proportion of bank loans in its portfolio is out of line with its desired portfolio composition, as explained in the next section. This is apt to happen when changes in portfolio size are dictated by reserve stringency or excess. The moves the bank takes to meet reserve requirements change its asset composition and thus affect the asset composition of the financial intermediary, which in turn affects the interest rates for those securities in which the financial intermediary makes a market.

Excess Reserves, Bills, and Bonds

The bank, after altering its outstanding bonded indebtedness and discounting, knows the total value of the assets with which it will end the round. These have been changed during the round by changes in the bank's liabilities. It next must decide the desired distribution of its portfolio among reserves, bills, bonds, mortgages, and loans. This allocation is done in a manner similar to the portfolio-allocation decision of nonfinancial firms (see chapter 4). Unlike these other firms, however, the bank cannot directly adjust the actual to the desired level of all of its financial assets, since it is programmed to meet the demand for business and consumer loans at whatever interest rate it sets. It also is unable to change the level of its reserve holdings—the situation in which the U.S. banking system finds itself despite the ability of individual banks to alter their reserves. Thus, the model's bank can directly alter the levels of its holdings only of bills, bonds, and mortgages. Indirectly, it can try to alter its future holdings of loans by changing the interest rate on them.

We have programmed the bank (1) to calculate the quantity of excess reserves it desires to hold, (2) to calculate the fraction of the remainder of its portfolio, exclusive of required reserves, that it desires to allocate to each of the other financial assets, (3) to move its actual holdings of bills, bonds, and mortgages to the desired level, and (4) to adjust the bank-loan interest rate for the coming round as a function of the excess demand for loans.

The desired ratio of excess reserve holdings to total financial assets, DEXRES, is a function of the treasury-bill rate, RBIL, a proxy for the cost of holding these excess reserves:

$$\text{DEXRES} = a(1) + a(2)*\text{RBIL}. \tag{6.4}$$

From its total financial assets, the bank deducts its required reserves and desired excess reserves to get the size of the portfolio over which it wishes to allocate bills, bonds, mortgages, and consumer and business loans. The weight allocated to security I, WEIGHT(I), depends on the current rate of return on the asset, RETURN(I); the change in the return, CHGRET(I), a proxy for the expected capital gain or loss from holding the asset; and TIME.[5] Specifically:

$$\text{WEIGHT(I)} = a(\text{I}) + b(\text{I})*\text{RETURN(I)} + c(\text{I})*\text{CHGRET(I)} \atop + d(\text{I})*\text{time}. \tag{6.5}$$

Table 6.2 gives the coefficient estimates for equation 6.5.

The WEIGHT(I) of an asset is set to zero if it has a negative value. The positive weights are then normalized to sum to one. The negative signs on some of the coefficients for rate of return reflect the fact that (1) the weights must add to one and (2) the returns on the various assets are highly correlated. In times of high interest rates, the bank wants to shift toward business and consumer loans. As a result of being unable to alter its holdings of loans directly, the bank may hold undesired excess reserves; the excess is allocated to bill and bond holdings, proportionally. Finally, purchases or sales are made to bring holdings of bills, bonds, and mortgages to the desired levels.

Setting the Interest Rate on Bank Loans

The current bank-loan rate charged to business firms, RBLO, is adjusted:

$$\text{RBLO} = a(1) + a(2)*\text{AVRBIL} + a(3)*\frac{\text{ABLOAN} - \text{DBLOAN}}{\text{DBLOAN}}, \tag{6.6}$$

Table 6.2. Parameters of bank demand for financial assets

Asset	Intercept	Return	Change in Return	Time	AAPE[a]	$\bar{R}^2$
Treasury	0.0639	−0.2512		−0.0000150	16.2	.37
bills	(15.69)	(−3.49)		(−2.09)		
Bonds	0.5566	−0.6896	−0.1347	0.0000460	1.68	.71
	(27.68)	(−1.213)	(−3.72)	(1.78)		
Mortgages	0.0736	−0.8461	0.1441	0.0000280	4.40	.34
	(3.84)	(−2.05)	(3.73)	(1.20)		
Business	0.2272	0.2836		−0.0000038	3.15	.37
loans	(44.50)	(5.61)		(−3.48)		
Consumer	0.07298	0.719		0.0000280	1.92	.73
loans	(5.17)	(5.37)		(8.98)		

NOTE: t-statistics are in parentheses.
[a]Average absolute percentage error.

where AVRBIL is a moving average of the treasury-bill rate, ABLOAN is the bank's actual business loans, and DBLOAN the desired level.

Each round, the bank sets the current interest rate on consumer loans, RCONS:

$$\text{RCONS} = a(1) + a(2)*\text{AVRBLO} + a(3)*\frac{\text{ACLOAN} - \text{DCLOAN}}{\text{DCLOAN}}, \quad (6.7)$$

where AVRBLO is a moving average of the bank-loan rate for businesses, ACLOAN is the bank's consumer loans, and DCLOAN the desired level.

Setting the Interest Rate on Savings Accounts

The bank sets the interest rate on savings accounts, RSAVAC, at a level depending on a moving average, AVRBIL, of the treasury-bill rate, and TIME:[6]

$$\text{RSAVAC} = a(1) + a(2)*\text{AVRBIL} + a(3)*\text{TIME}. \quad (6.8)$$

The Financial Intermediary

The financial intermediary represents the insurance industry, securities brokers and dealers, and other nonbank financial firms (except savings institutions). In the national accounts, it corresponds to the portion of the finance, insurance, and real-estate industry that remains after excluding banking and real estate. The firm has an output of financial services, which it sells to other actors (see table 6.1), and it maintains a work force and plant and equipment largely financed by bond issues. Households buy services from the financial intermediary in a fashion similar to their purchases of other firms' nondurable output. Other firms buy a fixed quantity of these services per physical unit of production and per physical unit of investment.

The financial intermediary performs a key function in the model—it makes a market in all open-market securities by announcing a yield to maturity for each type of security at the beginning of each round and by purchasing all securities offered and selling all securities demanded at these yields during the round. It also acts on behalf of the other actors who own assets, holding for them the record of all of their financial claims (except deposits and bank-loan instruments), collecting the flows of interest and dividend payments, and disbursing the appropriate share of such payments to each asset holder.

Market Making

The open market instruments (differentiated by maturity, IMAT) in which the financial intermediary makes a market are

1. Mortgages: HMORT(IMAT); IMAT $= 1,300$.
2. Longer-term federal government bonds: BONDS(IGOVF,IMAT); IMAT $=$ 13,180.
3. Treasury bills: BLOANS(IGOVF,IMAT) and BONDS(IGOVF,IMAT); IMAT $=$ 1,12.
4. Municipal bonds: BONDS(IGOVO,IMAT); IMAT $= 1,180$.
5. Private business bonds: BONDS(IFIRM,IMAT); IFIRM $= 1,12$; IMAT $=$ 1,180.

Mortgages, which originate in loans made by the financial intermediary to home-buying households, are held only by the bank, the federal government, and by the financial intermediary. The other assets in the list above (the open-market securities of chapters 4 and 5) are held by all of the nongovernmental actors. The financial intermediary routinely buys any newly issued open-market security of whatever type from its issuer on the occasion of its issuance. When it sells assets to nonbank investors (or buys them back), it does so by selling or buying shares of its portfolio of all open-market assets in existence (all of which are held in the street name of the financial intermediary in any case).

The financial intermediary holds a portfolio of assets on its own account, partly as a buffer stock for its market-making activities, partly for its insurance business, and partly as an investment. When orders from other actors to sell a particular debt instrument do not equal orders to buy, the amount of that instrument held in the portfolio of the financial intermediary expands or contracts accordingly. A surge in demand for treasury bills, which are traded in large quantities between the bank and the financial intermediary, could wipe out its buffer stock. In this case, the financial intermediary can sell short.[7]

While its actual portfolio is subject to the desires of the other actors, the financial intermediary has in mind at all times a desired portfolio. Its decision-making routine with respect to this portfolio is parallel to that of the nonfinancial firms (chapter 4). The amount of an asset the financial intermediary desires to hold depends on its portfolio size and on the asset's return and change in return. As is true for the bank, the major difference between the financial intermediary and nonfinancial firms is that, if the former finds itself with a portfolio out of line with its desired size and composition, it cannot effectuate its desires directly by sales to or purchases from other actors. Because of its market-making role, it must operate indirectly by changing interest rates, thus hoping to induce purchases or sales by the other actors, which will bring its own portfolio into line. An undesired overstock (measured at maturity value) of a particular financial instrument causes the financial intermediary to raise the interest rate in the next round for that instrument, while an understock will cause it to lower the interest rate.

Issuing Its Own Bonds

The financial intermediary issues bonds in all respects similar to those issued by nonfinancial firms (see chapter 4). The desired ratio, DEBTR, of the outstanding stock of these bonds to the financial intermediary's financial assets is given by

$$\text{DEBTR} = a(1) + a(2)*(\text{RBON} - \text{RLOAN}) + a(3)*\text{TIME}. \qquad (6.9)$$

Adjusting the Portfolio

At this point, the financial intermediary has completed all of its participation in the markets for goods and services, has serviced its debt, and has issued any bonds it wished to issue. All other actors have completed all of their transactions. The financial intermediary surveys this situation and decides on its desired total of bank-loan liabilities, depending on its sales and on interest rates:

$$\begin{aligned}\text{DLOANR} = \ &\text{AVSALE(IOFI)}*\text{P(IOFI)} \\ &*[a(1) + a(2)*\text{RLONG}(180) + a(3)*\text{TIME}].\end{aligned} \qquad (6.10)$$

The financial intermediary now knows its desired portfolio size. It decides the desired share in this portfolio of each financial asset by calculating the desired weight for each security, WEIGHT(I), as a function of its return, RET(I), change in return, CHGRET(I), and TIME:

$$\begin{aligned}\text{WEIGHT(I)} = \ &a(\text{I}) + b(\text{I})*\text{RET(I)} + c(\text{I})*\text{CHGRET(I)} \\ &+ d(\text{I})*\text{TIME}.\end{aligned} \qquad (6.11)$$

Table 6.3. Parameters of financial intermediary demand for financial assets

Asset	Intercept	Return	Change in Return	Time	AAPE[a]	$\bar{R}^2$
Cash	0.04732			−0.000027	4.43	.83
	(76.13)			(−15.75)		
Treasury	0.00737	−0.0236		0.0000093	16.16	.44
bills	(8.87)	(−1.61)		(6.23)		
Bonds	0.8084	−0.7858	0.0174	0.000261	0.34	.99
	(89.15)	−(3.07)	(1.07)	(22.19)		
Mortgages	0.1357	0.4450	−0.01267	−0.00023	3.55	.99
	(22.59)	(3.43)	(−1.047)	(−32.05)		

NOTE: t-statistics are in parentheses.
[a]Average absolute percentage error.

Parameters for this equation are presented in table 6.3. As in the case of the portfolio weights used by the bank, the negative coefficients on rate of return represent a desire to shift away from some assets in periods of high interest rates (see note 5). Negative WEIGHT(I) are set to zero, and the positive weights are normalized to sum to one. Through repaying debts or borrowing, the financial intermediary brings its cash account toward the desired level (it cannot repay more debt than it has). Finally, it notes the differences between its desired and actual holdings of bills, bonds, and mortgages for use in setting their interest rates.

Setting Market Interest Rates

The financial intermediary then adjusts interest rates on treasury bills as a function of the expected inflation rate, EXPINF (a moving average of price changes); time; and its own overstock of bills relative to aggregate bills. The rates on federal government bonds and on mortgages are adjusted depending on a moving average, AVRBIL, of the bill rate and on the financial intermediary's overstock of the asset relative to the aggregate of that asset:

$$\text{RBIL} = a(1) + a(2)*\text{EXPINF} \qquad (6.12)$$
$$+ \ a(3)*\text{TIME} + a(4)*\frac{\text{ACTBIL} - \text{DESBIL}}{\text{SUMBIL}},$$

$$\text{RBON} = a(1) + a(2)*\text{AVRBIL} \qquad (6.13)$$
$$+ \ a(3)*\text{TIME} + a(4)*\frac{\text{ACTBON} - \text{DESBON}}{\text{SUMBON}},$$

$$\text{RMOR} = a(1) + a(2)*\text{AVRBIL} \qquad (6.14)$$
$$+ \ a(3)*\text{TIME} + a(4)*\frac{\text{ACTMOR} - \text{DESMOR}}{\text{SUMOR}},$$

where the prefix SUM indicates the aggregate amount of the asset held by all actors.

The current bond rate of the firms is now set as a multiple of RBON, which incorporates a risk premium for these bonds over federal governments bonds. The state/local government's bond rate, RMUNI, is set to maintain its initial value relative to the federal government bond rate. Any treasury bond with more than one quarter to run is sold at a price yielding the same rate of return as a newly issued bond, and the firms' bonds also are priced in this way. The simulated curve of yield against maturity date is thus a step function with but two steps, the bill rate and a single bond rate.

Chapter 7. The Governments and the Monetary Authority

In this chapter, we review the activities of the model's federal government, state/local government (representing all of the state and local governments of the United States), and the monetary authority (representing the Federal Reserve Board and a considerable number of other U.S. agencies, such as the Federal Home Loan Bank Board, which influence one or another aspect of the money market). Many activities reviewed in this chapter are described in earlier chapters as they impinge on households, nonfinancial firms, and the bank and financial intermediary; but this chapter provides a summary of them.

The governmental actors purchase labor from households and buy goods and services from the firms in order to produce services presumably desired by the citizenry; they must manage their debt and collect the legislated taxes. The federal government also has the potential of subsidizing persons and activities and of forbidding some kinds of economic behavior and mandating other kinds. These activities affect the distribution of income, the price level, the composition of output, and the aggregate level of economic activity.

Because we conceive governmental actors on the federal level to be self-consciously interested in the effect of their actions on the entire economic system and to have certain aims respecting the path the system takes, the federal government and the monetary authority have a special place in the model. A major purpose of building any economic model is, of course, to diagnose effects of various policies on the path of the system. The present model provides new opportunities for realistic representation of policies and for calculating in detail their effects on the income flows and balance sheets of the actors. It also permits a calculation of the effect of any policy change on the distribution of income. For each of the policy instruments discussed below, we give a brief synopsis of how the direct and indirect effects of a change in that instrument are represented by the model.

A large number of magnitudes (tax rates, discount rates, interest ceilings, and so on) controlled by the government and the monetary authority are customarily considered instruments of policy. In any run of the model, a time series of values of each of the instruments must be provided, so that the actors know what taxes to pay, and so on. These time series can be generated in a number of ways, each way being appropriate to a particular research objective.

One way to generate such values is a fully exogenous method: the actual values historically assumed by policy-instrument variables are provided to the actors. This method is appropriate for estimating parameter values. A second method of assigning values to these variables is the fully endogenous method. It is possible to contrive behavioral specifications so that activities of the policy-oriented actors are as endogenous to the model as those of the other actors, using either those rules that in actuality governed past policy or some seemingly desirable set of rules that might be applied in the future.

We consider it inappropriate to use the fully exogenous method for runs of the model that purport to represent the way things would have gone in a historical period had certain elements of the situation been different than they in fact were. Had important endogenous variables such as the unemployment rate, the inflation rate, or the federal deficit been considerably different, the policy-oriented actors would, presumably, have acted differently. In order to meet the need to represent the variation in governmental behavior that would have occurred in such cases, we have not attempted to develop a fully blown endogenous structure, which would have required the formulation and testing of hypotheses concerning long-lived rules of behavior for the governmental actors in charge of policy. Rather, we developed a semiexogenous representation, which permitted what we considered to be a reasonable amount of flexibility in governmental behavior in response to circumstances departing from the historical record, but which kept the policy close to the track that it had followed in actuality. The reader will gain a more precise notion of this strategy in the discussion of the individual policy instruments that follows.

The Governments

In the course of each round, the major inflows and outflows of funds to and from governments take place in the following order (see chapter 2 for the description for all thirty-two events):

1. Interest paid and received on governments' liabilities and assets.
2. Taxes paid to governments by firms.

3. Wages paid to government employees.
4. Transfers paid by governments to households.
5. Taxes paid to governments by households.
6. Governments' purchases of goods and services from firms.
7. Governments' final financial adjustment.

In the course of any of the bouts of expenditures (1, 3, 4, and 6 above), a government may run out of cash. If it does, it automatically receives a loan from the bank. However, all of these loans are completely extinguished by the end of the round in the course of the governments' final financial adjustment. If, at that time, a government does not have on hand enough cash to extinguish its bank loans, it sells bonds or bills for cash to the financial intermediary, which floats them to the other actors but which in the interim may have to take out bank loans to accommodate the government. The governments' final financial adjustment, during which their bank loans are extinguished, occurs before the bank must examine its reserve position and before the financial intermediary sets new interest rates for the subsequent rounds.

The state/local government goes through each of the activities listed just after the federal government has gone through it.

Interest on Financial Assets and Liabilities

The governments pay interest on their outstanding debt each round. The federal government has as liabilities treasury bills, issued in the current round, IMAT $= 12$, or in the previous eleven rounds, which require interest payment when they mature at the original annual rate, RBILL(IMAT). Both governments also have as liabilities government bonds issued in the current month, IMAT $= 180$, or in the previous 179 months (one month consists of four rounds), which require interest payments each round at the original annual rate, RLONG(IMAT) in the case of the federal government; RMUNI(IMAT) in the case of state/local government. The state/local government issues only long-term debt.

The governments also receive interest payments on their portfolios of the obligations of other actors. Interest payments to the federal government are primarily on home mortgages and obligations of the agricultural sectors and the rest-of-world. The state/local government's assets primarily are the open-market securities held by its pension fund.

Setting Business Tax Rates

Industry-specific indirect business tax rates, TAXIND(IFIRM), are charged on sales of the products of the private firms. In the historical runs, these are set at the rates indicated in the national accounts. Data from the national accounts allow us to allocate the total of these taxes into the part paid to the federal government and the part paid to the state/local government, although not on an industry-specific basis. Property taxes paid by homeowners go to the state/local government. The fraction POL(14) of all other indirect business taxes paid to the federal government is set quarterly at the level indicated in the national accounts.

An increase in indirect business-tax rates for a firm immediately reduces government securities issues below what they would otherwise be and increases the cost of the firm's product to households. A fall in purchases of physical units of output by households then leads to employment losses, which partly offsets the government's sales-tax gain by an income-tax loss.

The federal corporate-profit tax rate, POL(8), and the state/local rate, POL(10), are set quarterly at the rates indicated in the national accounts. These rates are paid on the fraction of industry profits that are corporate profits, CORP(IFIRM). This magnitude is assumed to equal one for the bank and to be uniform for all other industries at a rate set exogenously with reference to the national accounts. The intricacy of corporate accounting for tax purposes, including depreciation allowances, has been subsumed under the average experienced and effective tax rate.

The immediate impact of lowering the effective corporate-profits tax rates is to increase government securities issues beyond what they would otherwise be and to increase firms' liquid-asset holdings. Second-order effects include an increase in dividend payments and, consequently, an increase in household saving and purchases.

Changes in the overall profits tax do not affect investment directly. However, the effect of an investment tax credit is to lower the price of capital goods (see chapter 4).

Governmental Enterprises

Government enterprises are such federal establishments as the postal service and the Tennessee Valley Authority and such state/local enterprises as transportation systems and lotteries. All of the government-enterprise flow-of-funds accounts are consolidated with those of the appropriate government. The same is true for employment and wage payments for government enterprises. Government enterprises purchase and hold inventories of supplies and finished products, produce for firms and for final demand, and price and deliver goods and services to firms and to final demand. Government enterprises are subject to neither capacity constraints nor labor-market constraints. Production and inventory adjustment occur for government enterprises in the same manner as for other firms. In historical runs, government-enterprise prices follow those for transportation and public utilities in

the national accounts. In counterfactual runs, they are set semiexogen-
ously—adjusted by the percentage by which the simulated GNP deflator
differs from the actual value.

Employment and Wages of Civil Servants

In runs of the model for past periods, the total labor employed by each
government sector, including government enterprises, can be set at the level
reported monthly by the Department of Labor, with employees apportioned
among the four occupations we distinguish and in the proportions that
prevailed in government sectors as reported in the Current Population Survey. Alternatively, any policy change that changes the level of government
employment, such as a public jobs program or an armed-forces buildup, can
be represented (see chapter 9). The governments participate in the hiring
hall, described in chapter 4.

Governments' wage-rate levels are based on governmental payroll
data reported in the national accounts. However, where appropriate, they
can be set by a semiexogenous process—adjusting the wage changes indicated by the national accounts by the percentage by which the simulated
average private-wage rate diverges from that reported for the United States
by the Department of Labor. This kind of adjustment allows us to simulate
the government wage bill in the counterfactual situations in which private
and public wages are above their historic values, as might occur if simulated
prices were above their historic levels.

Transfer Payments

The federal government each round makes transfers to firms and the rest-of-
world and gives grants-in-aid to state/local government in the amounts
indicated by the national accounts. Both governments pay welfare and
retirement benefits to the portion of the population not in the labor force, at
the average rate per person indicated in the national accounts. Were counterfactual policies that change welfare dependency to be simulated, appropriate changes in welfare payments could be made.

Unemployment insurance, UI, is in fact paid on a different formula by
each state. In the model, these differences are averaged out. Payments of UI
are made by the federal government to eligible unemployed members of the
labor force for up to twenty-five rounds at a fixed fraction of the worker's
usual wage rate, subject to a maximum that changes each year. The parameters that control the level of UI benefits are set to minimize the sum of
squared percentage deviations of the aggregate UI payments from the sum of
actual U.S. payments when unemployment is set exogenously.

Setting Personal Income Taxes

Personal income taxes are paid each round by each household. Where two members of the labor force are married, their income is pooled for tax purposes. Due to space limitations in computer core memory, we have not corrected explicitly for overpayments of taxes (due to progressivity) on the part of those with incomes that vary over the course of a calendar year.

The federal government sets six variables that determine the basic income taxes households pay:

POL(1):   The per-person exemption level, set in historical runs at the level that actually prevailed in the United States for the year in question.

POL(2):   The tax rate on the first dollar of taxable income.

POL(3):   The increment to the marginal tax rate per dollar of taxable income, set in historical runs at the increment in the actual tax rate for unmarried persons over the interval of taxable income from zero to $20,000.

POL(4):   The fraction of taxable income that is the standard deduction, taken from the tax tables.

POL(5):   The maximum standard deduction, taken from the tax tables.

POL(17):   The maximum tax rate on earned income.

These exemptions, deductions, and tax rates apply to both earned income and property income. The weekly income-tax bill for each worker (with appropriate adjustments for couples) is computed using the above statutory rates and then adjusted by a multiplicative factor to minimize the sum of squared deviations of the model's quarterly aggregate personal income taxes, from personal tax and nontax liability totals in the national income accounts.

Events like once-for-all rebates are easy to include. The income-tax rebate of 1975 was represented by reducing the worker's weekly federal income-tax bill by 40 percent (10 percent of estimated annual taxes) during the second quarter of 1975, subject to a maximum weekly tax reduction of $400.00/12.

Changes that raise the amount of taxes paid by a worker have the immediate effect of reducing that worker's disposable income, purchases of consumer goods and services, saving, and the stock of liquid assets; the rise in taxes also reduces new issues of federal government debt. Second-order effects include a reduction in the availability of mortgage money, possibly lowered production schedules, and possible delays in price rises. The latter two effects depend on the state of inventories and the general trend in business activity.

Personal income taxes are paid to the state/local government in the amount POL(6) times the worker's federal tax bill before rebates, if any. In historical runs, POL(6) is reset when the national accounts indicate a change in the ratio of federal to state/local income taxes.

Setting Social-Insurance Taxes

Two magnitudes set by statute govern the amount of social-insurance taxes: POL(9), the rate at which wages are taxed for the primary social-insurance program; and POL(7), the maximum individual income subject to social-insurance tax on a per-round basis. A multiplicative constant adjusts for incomplete coverage and overpayments of some workers employed part of the year, as reflected in the national accounts.[1]

The immediate effects of increasing the social-insurance tax are in the same direction as those caused by a rise in the income tax, but the greater regressivity of the social-insurance tax affects the magnitude of the effects.

For the contribution to federal social insurance by private employers, POL(7) and POL(9) are applied to the average weekly wage paid, WAGEF(ICASTE,IFIRM), which varies by type of worker and by firm. This contribution is adjusted by a multiplicative constant that minimizes the squared percentage deviations of simulated from quarterly values reported in the national accounts.

The immediate impact of raising employer contributions is: (1) to raise marginal and average production costs, thus increasing the likelihood that prices will be raised; (2) to raise the cost of labor relative to capital, thus ultimately increasing somewhat the rate at which old capital will be replaced; and (3) to increase federal government cash receipts, thus reducing new issues of government securities.

Purchases from Firms

The governments' desired spending for individual commodities in historical runs is obtained by allocating the particular government's spending for the separate categories of durables, nondurables, construction, and services indicated in the national accounts, among the various firms in the fixed proportions indicated in the 1972 input/output table for federal and state/local government purchases. The physical quantity of goods purchased from a firm is determined by dividing the spending for purchases from the firm by the appropriate price deflator.

In runs with counterfactual conditions, government spending diverges from historic values when endogenously determined firm-specific prices differ from historic prices. We assume that these price divergences cause no change in physical quantities purchased and that any costs or savings are absorbed fully by changes in the deficit rather than by endogenous adjustments of quantities purchased or by tax policy.

Adjusting the Portfolios

Each round, the federal government retires its maturing obligations—maturing bills, BLOANS(IGOVF,1), and one-fourth of the value of bonds maturing in the current month, BONDS(IGOVF,1). It does this by paying cash to the financial intermediary, borrowing the cash through bank loans if necessary.

Next, the federal government adjusts its holdings of home mortgages, BMORTG, to the level indicated in the flow-of-funds accounts by purchasing them for cash from the financial intermediary.[2] Increases in government holdings free the funds of private financial institutions for commitments to purchase mortgages for new construction. Changes in these home-mortgage holdings are an important policy instrument, both in the real economy of the United States and in the model.

Next, the federal government brings its ownership of bonds issued by nongovernmental actors, BBONDS(IGOVF), to the level indicated in the flow-of-funds accounts, again by purchases from the financial intermediary for cash. These are primarily obligations of the rest-of-world and of the agricultural firm.

The federal government has made all payments to the other actors out of its stock of cash, where that has been possible, and out of the proceeds of loans from the bank, where that was necessary. In the actual U.S. economy, the government avoids resorting to bank loans by timely issuance of bills, but in writing the program for the model, we found it convenient to allow the government to follow the routine set for all the other actors—to finance cash deficits during a round with bank loans. In the case of the government, all of these loans are extinguished at the end of the round through the issuance of bonds and bills, and this occurs before the point in the round at which the bank must meet reserve requirements.[3]

New bills and an exogenous quantity of new bonds are issued in sufficient aggregate to retire the bank loans contracted during the round and also to bring the federal government's cash account, CASH(IGOVF), to the level indicated as appropriate by the flow-of-funds accounts.[4] If, because of counterfactual policies, the simulated deficit differs from the actual U.S. deficit, the simulated bill and bond issuances will of course both differ from the actual.[5]

The portfolio-adjustment process of the federal government provides an important link between fiscal and monetary policy. An increase in federal tax receipts, for instance, reduces government issues of bills and bonds, which in turn causes the financial intermediary to set a lower bill and bond rate than it otherwise would. If the monetary authority is following a strategy of reaching interest-rate targets, the lower bill rate might cause it to change the discount rate and the magnitude of its open-market operations.

The final financial adjustment of the state/local government is entirely analogous to that programmed for the federal government.[6]

The Monetary Authority

Monetary and credit policy are determined by the monetary authority. The policy instruments at its disposal are

1. Required reserve ratios for savings accounts: at commercial banks, POL (22); at savings institutions, POL(30).
2. Maximum interest rate for savings accounts, POL(23).
3. Required down payment for home purchases, POL(18).
4. Required reserve ratio for demand deposits, POL(21).
5. Discount rate, RDIS.
6. Open-market operations.

Required Reserve Ratios for Savings Accounts

In the United States, savings accounts are liabilities of commercial banks and savings institutions, primarily savings and loan associations. The Federal Reserve sets the required reserve percentages for member banks, while the Federal Home Loan Bank Board sets it for federal savings and loan associations. The reserves for savings accounts at commercial banks are required to be held in the form of a deposit at the Federal Reserve, while the reserves required of savings institutions are held as deposits at commercial banks. The only function of the latter is to regulate the division of the savings institutions' portfolios between liquid assets and mortgages.

In the model, this complex reality has been simplified considerably. All savings accounts require reserves held at the monetary authority, and a single required ratio, POL(22), applies to them all. POL(30) is the fraction of savings institutions' deposits that can be invested in home mortgages.

Maximum Interest Rate for Savings Accounts

Historically in the United States, federal agencies have set maximum interest rates on various categories of savings accounts, including the rates permitted for savings institutions.[7] Usually, the rate permitted for savings institutions is somewhat higher than that for commercial banks. In the model, the monetary authority sets one maximum rate, POL(23), for all savings accounts, and this is set to approximate the average maximum permitted historically. In periods of high interest rates, this policy variable powerfully affects the level of investment in residences. When yields on open-market securities continue to rise while the rate on savings accounts is at a maximum, the actors shift more and more funds out of savings accounts and into open-market securities. This reduces the ability of the savings institution to commit funds for home mortgages, thus reducing housing starts.

Required Down Payment for Home Purchases

POL(18) is the fraction of the cost of a home that can be financed by issuing a home mortgage. In the United States, this is set by the Federal Housing Administration. Lowering POL(18) raises the quantity of home construction that can be financed with a given quantity of funds available to the financial system, but will prevent some prospective purchasers with too small a stock of assets for the down payment from acquiring a home.

Required Reserve Ratio for Demand Deposits

The monetary authority sets a uniform required reserve ratio, POL(21), for demand deposits. The model is a simplification of the U.S. economy in a number of details:

1. In the model, all money is treated as a deposit liability of the bank. In the U.S. economy, some money is a currency liability of the Federal Reserve and the U.S. Treasury.
2. In the model, all required reserves must be held as a deposit at the monetary authority. In the U.S. economy, vault cash is counted.
3. U.S. reserve requirements vary by size of bank and membership in the Federal Reserve system. The model has only one bank, whose reserve requirements are a weighted average.

In correcting for these simplicities of the model, the historic values of POL(21) are set each quarter by taking the required reserve ratio for the largest class of banks as set by the Federal Reserve Board and adjusted by a multiplicative factor.

Discount Rate and Discount Policy

In attempting to simulate the historical past, the discount rate that prevailed in the United States is used. However, for simulations of alternative policies, the discount rate is determined by those variables that influence the Federal Reserve in actually setting it. In such runs the monetary authority changes the rate charged on loans of reserves to the bank, RDIS, in response to a geometrically weighted moving average of the treasury-bill rate, AVRBIL:

$$\text{RDIS} = \text{RDIS}_o - .0025$$
$$\text{(if RDIS} > \text{AVRBIL} + \text{POL(27))}.$$
$$\text{RDIS} = \text{RDIS}_o + .0025$$
$$\text{(if RDIS} < \text{AVRBIL. Otherwise,}$$
$$\text{RDIS} = \text{RDIS}_o.$$

This formulation has the effect of moving the discount rate relatively infrequently.

Open-Market Operations

The heart of the short-run operation of monetary policy—in the model as in the real U.S. economy—is open-market operations. These are conducted in each round by the monetary authority after all sectors have completed their transactions on goods and services markets and after all sectors except the bank have fully adjusted their portfolios for the round. The monetary authority computes the reserves it desires the bank to have, DRESER, and then engages in open-market operations by transactions with the financial intermediary to bring actual reserves, RESERV, to the desired quantity.

The monetary authority can formulate its desired reserves in three different ways, depending on the purpose for which the model is being used. The simplest is for the authority to set DRESER at the actual level of reserves that prevailed historically in the United States. This formulation of DRESER, representing a fully exogenous monetary authority, is appropriate for fitting parameters of the model and to some extent for computing *ceteris paribus* multipliers.

A somewhat more endogenous formulation equates DRESER with the quantity of reserves required by the bank, RESREQ, plus the quantity of excess or free reserves that the Federal Reserve in actuality provided.

A third, more fully endogenous method of setting the level of desired reserves is for the monetary authority to set a target for the growth of reserves, shaded upward if it wants to stimulate the economy and shaded downward if it wants to cool the economy. Both unemployment rates and price movements presumably influence the monetary authority's perception of what direction to go, although its reaction to price movements is complicated by its desire to accommodate at least partially to exogenous cost-push elements, such as foreign oil-price movements. If the monetary authority wants to maintain orderly credit markets, interest-rate developments might also influence how heavily it shades growth rates up or down. (Craine, Havenner, and Berry [1978] have found that the Federal Reserve's provision of reserves can be described rather handily in this manner. The present model can be used to explore the results of varying rules for the Federal Reserve; see Bennett and Bergmann [1980].)

Chapter 8. Performance
of the Model

In a number of important senses, the Transactions Model is more lifelike than conventional macroeconomic models, which consist of simultaneous equations fit to quarterly macroeconomic data. As we have seen in previous chapters, prominent features of the model include the financial portrayal of individuals and businesses, the attention to money flows, the combination of fixed capital and labor in the production process, the replacement of simultaneity with recursiveness, and the replacement of the calendar quarter by the week as the shortest period within which a change in plans can take place.

However, for some purposes, the most important sense in which a model might be lifelike is in its ability to track macrodata for past periods and, what is not quite the same, its ability to predict well. It is probably fair to say that macroeconomists have improved their models' delineation of economic functioning (usually through added equations and variables) mainly to improve their predictive power. For a given degree of predictive reliability, parsimony of equations has been considered a virtue.

In building the Transactions Model, our aim was a more faithful delineation of the economic process and of the policy options available to affect that process. But we also attempted, for obvious reasons, to produce a model that behaves in a lifelike fashion on the macroeconomic level when run for past periods and that promises predictive power.

As explained in chapter 3, the assignment of numerical values to parameters was done by a method analogous to the equation-by-equation method ordinarily used to fit most large macroeconomic models. Param-

eters appearing in each of the twelve modules delineating behavior were
fitted under the assumption that the other modules were behaving so as to
track exactly the macrodata they directly affect. Some of the parameter
values came from conventional regressions on macrodata, others were
extraneous, and others were arrived at by iterative search; that is, by rerunning the model with different sets of parameter values until a fit to a
specified tolerance was achieved.

After a complete set of parameters had been developed, each module
was tested by being run in endogenous mode for the period 1967–79, with
all of the other modules in exogenous mode, that is, forced to track the

Table 8.1. Mean errors for major macroeconomic variables

Variable	1977–78		1980–81	
	Quarter	Two-Year	Quarter	Two-Year
Gross national product[a]	−31.0	−58.0	−41.0	69.0
	(1.40)	(2.86)	(1.67)	(2.48)
Real GNP[b]	−17.0	−25.0	5.0	38.0
	(1.44)	(1.93)	(0.87)	(2.14)
GNP deflator[c]	0.0	−1.0	−3.0	1.0
	(0.34)	(0.91)	(1.78)	(0.85)
Consumer price index[c]	−1.0	−2.0	0.0	4.0
	(0.17)	(1.10)	(0.28)	(1.86)
Compensation of employees[a]	−2.0	−17.0	−1.0	0.0
	(0.23)	(1.38)	(0.10)	(0.27)
Civilian unemployment rate[d]	0.4	1.1	0.2	−0.6
	(5.25)	(17.70)	(3.72)	(8.00)
Personal consumption expenditures[a]	10.9	4.0	−19.0	15.0
	(1.83)	(2.09)	(1.19)	(1.07)
Fixed investment[a]	−15.0	−39.0	−10.0	45.0
	(4.23)	(11.0)	(3.01)	(10.5)
Treasury-bill rate[e]	0.4	0.1	−1.7	−0.8
	(10.5)	(10.4)	(19.5)	(18.4)
Treasury-bond rate[e]	−0.1	0.0	−1.7	−1.7
	(2.10)	(2.28)	(15.6)	(15.3)
Mortgage rate[e]	−0.1	0.1	−2.0	−2.0
	(1.52)	(2.08)	(13.6)	(13.0)
Bank-loan rate[e]	−0.2	0.0	−0.7	−0.5
	(4.5)	(6.44)	(12.47)	(12.5)
Money supply (M2)[a]	7.0	−23.0	−5.0	−44.0
	(1.0)	(1.6)	(0.9)	(2.6)

NOTE: Average absolute percentage errors are in parentheses.
[a]Billions of dollars, seasonally adjusted annual rate.
[b]Billions of 1972 dollars, seasonally adjusted annual rate.
[c]1972 = 100
[d]Percent.
[e]Annual percentage rate.

Table 8.2. Gross national product (billions of dollars, seasonally adjusted annual rate)

Quarter	1977–78			1980–81		
		Predicted			Predicted	
	Actual	Quarter	Two-Year	Actual	Quarter	Two-Year
1	1835	1846	1846	2576	2584	2594
2	1895	1862	1870	2573	2579	2657
3	1954	1918	1914	2644	2629	2746
4	1989	1960	1958	2739	2673	2810
5	2032	2016	2007	2865	2781	2902
6	2139	2069	2053	2902	2855	2977
7	2202	2175	2077	2981	2902	3039
8	2282	2276	2146	3003	2936	3111
Mean	2041	2015	1983	2785	2744	2854
AAPE[a]		1.4	2.9		1.7	2.5

[a]Average absolute percentage error.

macrodata. In these runs, errors were allowed to cumulate in both the microaccounts and macroaccounts, and structural and parameter changes were made if the module produced macroestimates that ran seriously off the track.

The values of the parameters fitted by this long and rather variegated process, with an indication of the methodology, t-statistics, and $\bar{R}$-squares, are shown in the appendix. As is obvious, the fits to the macrodata are

Table 8.3. Real gross national product (billions of 1972 dollars, seasonally adjusted annual rate)

Quarter	1977–78			1980–81		
		Predicted			Predicted	
	Actual	Quarter	Two-Year	Actual	Quarter	Two-Year
1	1341	1350	1350	1495	1514	1514
2	1363	1340	1349	1458	1485	1516
3	1386	1359	1364	1464	1478	1527
4	1389	1365	1374	1479	1466	1519
5	1400	1381	1387	1508	1495	1528
6	1437	1395	1391	1502	1505	1526
7	1449	1436	1395	1510	1502	1518
8	1468	1472	1421	1490	1496	1511
Mean	1404	1387	1379	1488	1493	1520
AAPE[a]		1.4	1.9		0.9	2.1

[a]Average absolute percentage error.

Table 8.4. Gross national product deflator

Quarter	1977–78 Actual	1977–78 Predicted Quarter	1977–78 Predicted Two-Year	1980–81 Actual	1980–81 Predicted Quarter	1980–81 Predicted Two-Year
1	137	137	137	172	171	171
2	139	139	139	177	174	175
3	141	141	140	181	178	180
4	143	144	142	185	182	185
5	145	146	145	190	186	190
6	149	148	147	193	190	195
7	152	151	149	197	193	200
8	155	155	151	202	196	206
Mean	145	145	144	187	184	188
AAPE[a]		0.3	0.9		1.8	0.9

NOTE: 1972 = 100.

[a]Average absolute percentage error.

generally fair to middling, and some are downright poor by the standards economists have achieved in fitting macroeconomic equations. However, more important than the fit of the individual equations is the behavior of the model when all of the parts are allowed to operate together and interact. It is this latter kind of behavior that is reported on in this chapter.

If the model is to be useful for policy studies, it must give reasonably

Table 8.5. Consumer price index

Quarter	1977–78 Actual	1977–78 Predicted Quarter	1977–78 Predicted Two-Year	1980–81 Actual	1980–81 Predicted Quarter	1980–81 Predicted Two-Year
1	136	136	136	168	168	168
2	138	138	137	172	171	172
3	140	140	139	176	175	177
4	142	142	141	180	179	182
5	144	144	143	183	183	186
6	147	147	145	187	186	192
7	150	149	147	190	190	197
8	153	152	149	193	193	203
Mean	144	143	142	181	181	185
AAPE[a]		0.2	1.1		0.3	1.9

NOTE: 1972 = 100.

[a]Average absolute percentage error.

Table 8.6. Compensation of employees (billions of dollars, seasonally adjusted annual rate)

	1977–78			1980–81		
		Predicted			Predicted	
Quarter	Actual	Quarter	Two-Year	Actual	Quarter	Two-Year
1	1101	1100	1100	1555	1549	1549
2	1136	1133	1125	1572	1572	1572
3	1168	1168	1157	1605	1604	1611
4	1203	1199	1196	1663	1662	1657
5	1238	1236	1227	1717	1718	1712
6	1283	1275	1257	1750	1748	1750
7	1320	1316	1284	1789	1788	1787
8	1363	1362	1325	1813	1812	1824
Mean	1226	1224	1209	1683	1682	1683
AAPE[a]		0.2	1.4		0.1	0.3

[a]Average absolute percentage error.

realistic results when run fully endogenously—with all of its modules in endogenous mode. When it is run this way, the errors of one module influence all the rest. To test the model, we ran it in fully endogenous mode for two periods: a two-year stretch late in the period of parameter estimation (1977–78), and a two-year stretch coming after the period of parameter estimation (1980–81). The runs for the latter period are analogous to predic-

Table 8.7. Unemployment rate (percentage)

	1977–78			1980–81		
		Predicted			Predicted	
Quarter	Actual	Quarter	Two-Year	Actual	Quarter	Two-Year
1	7.5	7.7	7.7	6.3	6.1	6.1
2	7.1	7.5	8.1	7.3	7.2	6.5
3	6.9	7.0	7.7	7.6	7.8	6.6
4	6.6	7.2	7.4	7.5	7.7	6.6
5	6.3	6.6	7.4	7.4	7.7	6.6
6	6.0	6.7	7.6	7.4	7.9	7.1
7	6.0	6.3	7.8	7.4	7.9	7.2
8	5.9	6.0	7.5	8.4	8.6	7.8
Mean	6.5	6.9	7.6	7.4	7.6	6.8
AAPE[a]		5.2	17.7		3.7	8.0

[a]Average absolute percentage error.

Table 8.8. Personal consumption expenditures (billions of dollars, seasonally adjusted annual rate)

		1977–78			1980–81	
		Predicted			Predicted	
Quarter	Actual	Quarter	Two-Year	Actual	Quarter	Two-Year
1	1163	1194	1194	1619	1609	1609
2	1187	1201	1202	1622	1625	1646
3	1216	1242	1250	1682	1689	1723
4	1252	1248	1255	1746	1703	1746
5	1276	1308	1313	1800	1771	1804
6	1331	1314	1298	1819	1801	1840
7	1367	1388	1335	1869	1844	1890
8	1411	1454	1382	1884	1848	1913
Mean	1275	1294	1279	1755	1736	1771
AAPE[a]		1.8	2.1		1.2	1.1

[a]Average absolute percentage error.

tion, except that the values of the exogenous variables were known and did not themselves have to be predicted.

For each time period, the model was run with all of its modules in endogenous mode. Runs using two distinct methods of dealing with errors were performed:

Table 8.9. Fixed investment (billions of dollars, seasonally adjusted annual rate)

		1977–78			1980–81	
		Predicted			Predicted	
Quarter	Actual	Quarter	Two-Year	Actual	Quarter	Two-Year
1	277	272	272	425	429	429
2	296	279	278	391	400	443
3	307	295	283	405	389	456
4	324	308	289	428	407	470
5	329	319	295	443	426	484
6	358	334	301	451	438	498
7	371	356	308	454	442	511
8	383	369	314	456	444	525
Mean	331	316	292	432	422	477
AAPE[a]		4.2	11.0		3.0	10.5

[a]Average absolute percentage error.

Table 8.10. Treasury bill rate (percentage)

		1977–78			1980–81	
		Predicted			Predicted	
Quarter	Actual	Quarter	Two-Year	Actual	Quarter	Two-Year
1	4.7	5.6	5.6	12.9	11.4	11.4
2	4.9	5.9	5.6	9.3	11.1	11.4
3	5.5	6.2	5.9	9.3	11.3	11.6
4	6.2	6.5	6.2	13.9	11.2	11.8
5	6.4	6.7	6.9	14.8	11.2	12.2
6	6.4	6.9	6.9	16.0	11.1	12.4
7	7.1	7.3	6.7	15.5	11.2	12.8
8	8.8	7.8	6.9	11.4	11.2	13.2
Mean	6.2	6.6	6.3	12.9	11.2	12.1
AAPE[a]		10.5	10.4		19.5	18.4

[a]Average absolute percentage error.

1. In one method, which might be described as a one-quarter-at-a-time method, we forced all microeconomic magnitudes at the beginning of each quarter to levels that conformed with the macroeconomic magnitudes indicated by the data for that point in time. The model was then run for the quarter following that point in time, consisting of twelve weeks or rounds, and the end-of-quarter simulated macroeconomic values were compared with the macroeconomic magnitudes indicated

Table 8.11. Treasury bond rate (percentage)

		1977–78			1980–81	
		Predicted			Predicted	
Quarter	Actual	Quarter	Two-Year	Actual	Quarter	Two-Year
1	6.2	6.1	6.1	10.0	8.3	8.3
2	6.3	6.1	6.2	8.6	8.6	8.4
3	6.1	6.2	6.3	9.2	8.5	8.6
4	6.2	6.3	6.4	10.3	8.4	8.7
5	6.6	6.5	6.6	10.7	8.7	8.8
6	6.9	6.6	6.7	11.3	8.9	8.9
7	6.9	6.8	6.8	11.9	9.1	9.0
8	7.1	7.0	6.8	11.2	9.2	9.2
Mean	6.5	6.4	6.5	10.4	8.7	8.7
AAPE[a]		2.1	2.3		15.5	15.3

[a]Average absolute percentage error.

Table 8.12. Mortgage rate (percentage)

| | | 1977–78 | | | 1980–81 | |
| | | Predicted | | | Predicted | |
Quarter	Actual	Quarter	Two-Year	Actual	Quarter	Two-Year
1	8.6	8.8	8.8	13.7	12.4	12.4
2	8.8	8.9	9.0	12.2	12.8	12.6
3	8.8	9.0	9.1	13.6	12.6	12.7
4	8.9	9.2	9.3	14.6	12.4	12.9
5	9.3	9.4	9.5	14.9	12.9	13.1
6	9.8	9.7	9.8	16.4	13.3	13.2
7	9.9	9.9	9.9	18.1	13.6	13.4
8	10.1	10.2	9.9	16.2	13.8	13.7
Mean	9.3	9.4	9.4	15.0	13.0	13.0
AAPE[a]		1.5	2.1		13.6	13.0

[a] Average absolute percentage error.

by the data. The microeconomic magnitudes were then corrected for the beginning of the next quarter, and the process continued.

2. The second method allowed full cumulation of the errors through time. The microeconomic magnitudes were set only once; namely for the initial conditions at the beginning of the period. A run of eight quarters, consisting of ninety-six rounds, was then made, with errors allowed to accumulate over the entire two-year period.

Table 8.13. Bank loan rate (percentage)

| | | 1977–78 | | | 1980–81 | |
| | | Predicted | | | Predicted | |
Quarter	Actual	Quarter	Two-Year	Actual	Quarter	Two-Year
1	9.3	9.9	9.9	23.4	22.6	22.6
2	9.5	10.0	10.3	24.5	24.3	23.3
3	10.1	10.4	10.8	16.6	23.2	23.9
4	11.5	10.8	11.2	24.0	22.2	24.3
5	11.8	11.7	12.2	28.7	24.3	25.0
6	12.3	12.6	13.0	28.9	25.6	25.5
7	13.4	13.4	13.3	30.3	26.7	26.1
8	16.2	14.3	13.4	25.0	27.4	26.9
Mean	11.8	11.6	11.8	25.2	24.5	24.7
AAPE[a]		4.5	6.4		12.5	12.5

[a] Average absolute percentage error.

Table 8.14. Money supply (M2; billions of dollars, end of period)

		1977–78			1980–81	
		Predicted			Predicted	
Quarter	Actual	Quarter	Two-Year	Actual	Quarter	Two-Year
1	1267	1262	1262	1689	1714	1714
2	1311	1306	1297	1744	1743	1743
3	1342	1344	1329	1793	1767	1765
4	1389	1380	1365	1860	1830	1794
5	1392	1410	1382	1889	1891	1827
6	1445	1448	1415	1938	1953	1879
7	1481	1512	1441	1997	2005	1938
8	1529	1568	1476	2064	2032	1963
Mean	1394	1401	1371	1872	1867	1828
AAPE[a]		1.0	1.6		.9	2.6

[a]Average absolute percentage error.

Summary statistics for these two kinds of runs for the two time periods are displayed in table 8.1. The table gives mean errors and average absolute percentage errors for thirteen major endogenous macroeconomic variables. Tables 8.2 through 8.14 give the patterns through time of the simulated and actual values, and figures 8.1 through 8.26 chart the time path of the errors. The major exogenous variables throughout are bank reserves, exports, imports, and government purchases of goods and services from each sector, including the households, which supply labor. The money supply is determined by the module controlling bank behavior.

The government deficit at any time depends on exogenous government purchases, the level of activity that controls tax collections and transfers, the predetermined national debt, (which in the two-year runs is subject to simulated additions), and the rate of interest, which affects the size of debt-service payments. The deficit in any round affects the supply of credit instruments in that round, and this in turn affects the interest rate set in the next round.

Looking overall at the predictions, we consider them to be remarkably good, despite obvious weak spots. The model's most notable achievement is the prediction of an upper turning point in real GNP in the two-year run for the 1980–81 period, six quarters after the start of the run. In actuality, the downturn came one quarter later.

As it stands, the model has a tendency to underpredict the level of activity, which is quite evident in the single-quarter predictions for the 1977–78 period. The unemployment rate is on average 0.4 percentage points high, real GNP is on average $17 billion too low, and the CPI is one

Table 8.15. Mean Errors for Microprices

ID Number	Firm[a]	1977–78		1980–81	
		Quarter	Two-Year	Quarter	Two-Year
3	Construction	1.40	−3.9	2.4	11.3
		(0.8)	(2.4)	(0.1)	(4.7)
4	Automobile manufacturing	0.70	0.8	−0.9	−14.5
		(0.8)	(1.5)	(1.4)	(7.6)
5	Other durable manufacturing	1.00	1.0	1.8	4.3
		(0.7)	(0.7)	(1.1)	(2.5)
6	Nondurable manufacturing	0.08	−1.7	3.6	16.3
		(0.6)	(1.2)	(2.1)	(9.4)
7	Capital-intensive services	1.10	2.6	3.1	6.6
		(0.8)	(1.9)	(1.8)	(3.7)
8	Trade	0.90	−0.3	1.8	3.8
		(0.6)	(0.5)	(1.0)	(2.1)
9	Other services	1.10	0.9	2.0	3.3
		(0.7)	(0.8)	(1.1)	(1.7)
10	Real estate	0.40	−4.0	2.5	10.7
		(0.3)	(2.9)	(1.4)	(6.0)

NOTE: Prices are endogenous only for the above industries. Average absolute percentage errors are in parentheses.
[a]See table 2.2 for definitions of firms.

Table 8.16. Mean errors for micro consumer expenditures

ID Number	Firm[a]	1977–78		1980–81	
		Quarter	Two-Year	Quarter	Two-Year
1	Agriculture	−0.1	−0.26	0.10	0.40
		(2.0)	(2.2)	(0.9)	(2.5)
4	Automobile manufacturing	−3.5	−3.90	−4.20	−1.80
		(22.0)	(23.0)	(16.0)	(13.0)
5	Other durable manufacturing	1.9	1.08	6.70	8.30
		(3.2)	(2.4)	(8.7)	(10.8)
6	Nondurable manufacturing	29.1	25.70	29.90	38.60
		(12.2)	(10.8)	(8.8)	(11.6)
7	Capital-intensive services	−2.0	−3.10	−10.20	−7.60
		(2.4)	(3.1)	(7.0)	(5.2)
8	Trade	6.1	3.00	7.60	15.90
		(2.7)	(2.4)	(2.4)	(5.0)
9	Other services	−14.5	15.30	−33.10	−29.80
		(4.8)	(5.0)	(7.8)	(7.0)

(*continued*)

Table 8.16. (*continued*)

ID Number	Firm[a]	1977–78		1980–81	
		Quarter	Two-Year	Quarter	Two-Year
10	Real estate	1.5	−2.20	−7.90	−2.30
		(1.5)	(2.1)	(3.0)	(1.0)
11	Financial intermediary	−1.3	−1.70	−5.30	−4.40
		(2.8)	(3.6)	(8.0)	(6.7)
12	Bank	2.0	2.00	1.80	2.00
		(6.0)	(5.8)	(3.9)	(4.3)
15	Rest-of-world	−2.4	−2.20	−4.63	−4.98
		(15.0)	(14.0)	(19.3)	(20.8)

NOTE: Expenditures are endogenous only for the above industries. Average absolute percentage errors are in parentheses.
[a]See table 2.2 for definitions of firms 1–12.

percentage point too low. The two-year predictions exacerbate this bias for this time period.

For the 1980–81 stretch, the model badly misses the volatility of interest rates, which the economy demonstrated in actuality. In this, it keeps company with other macroeconomic models. Of course, the October 1979 change in Federal Reserve behavior, which resulted in more volatile interest rates, came after our parameter estimation period. The underestimation of interest rates caused an overestimation of investment, particularly residential investment, which in turn caused overestimates in incomes, consumer expenditures, and consumer prices. Tables 8.15 and 8.16 give a picture of the performance of the Transactions Model in predicting microprices and consumer expenditures.

In hindsight, we can see that a number of easily accomplished alterations in the structure of the model would give interest rates greater volatility. To have made these alterations before reporting our results would have violated our self-imposed rule of reporting as our test of prediction our first run on data outside the period to which the model's parameters were fitted.

The fits obtained in these runs of the model, while leaving considerable room for improvement, are amply sufficient to lend weight and interest to the policy simulations reported on in the next chapter.

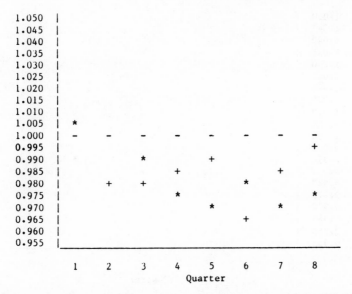

Figure 8.1. Gross National Product, Ratio of Quarter Predictions to Actual (1977–78 = +; 1980–81 = *)

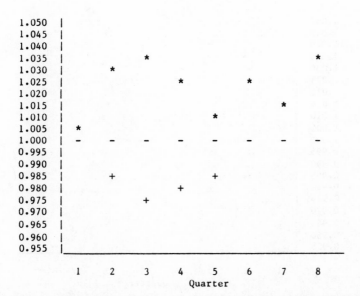

Figure 8.2. Gross National Product, Ratio of Two-Year Predictions to Actual (1977–78 = +; 1980–81 = *)

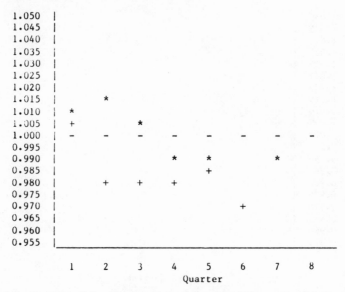

Figure 8.3.   Real Gross National Product, Ratio of Quarter Predictions to Actual (1977–78 = +; 1980–81 = ∗)

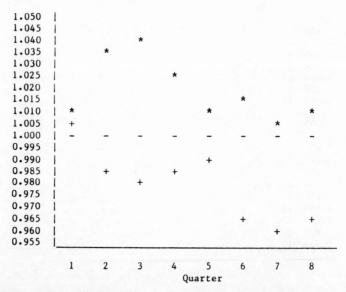

Figure 8.4.   Real Gross National Product, Ratio of Two-Year Predictions to Actual (1977–78 = +; 1980–81 = ∗)

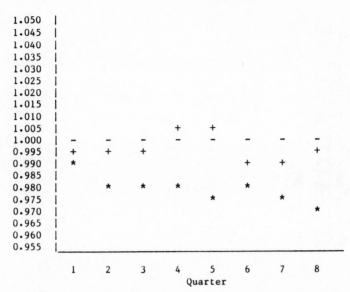

Figure 8.5.   GNP Deflator, Ratio of Quarter Predictions to Actual (1977–78 = +; 1980–81 = ∗)

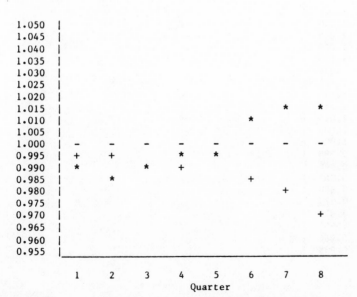

Figure 8.6.   GNP Deflator, Ratio of Two-Year Predictions to Actual (1977–78 = +; 1980–81 = ∗)

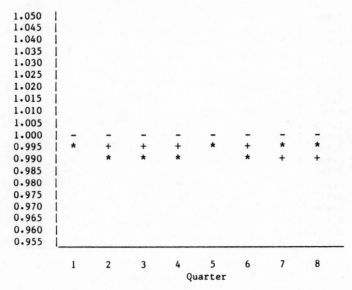

Figure 8.7. Consumer Price Index, Ratio of Quarter Predictions to Actual (1977–78 = +; 1980–81 = *)

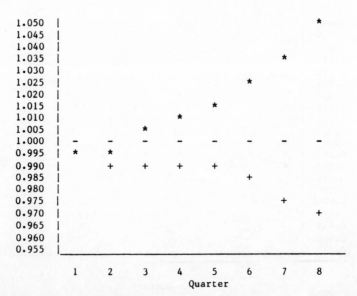

Figure 8.8. Consumer Price Index, Ratio of Two-Year Predictions to Actual (1977–78 = +; 1980–81 = *)

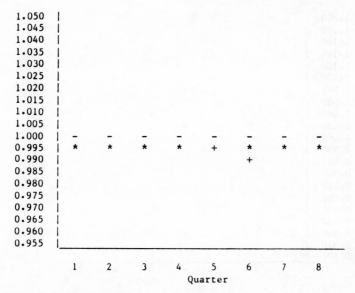

Figure 8.9. Compensation of Employees, Ratio of Quarter Predictions to Actual (1977–78 = +; 1980–81 = *)

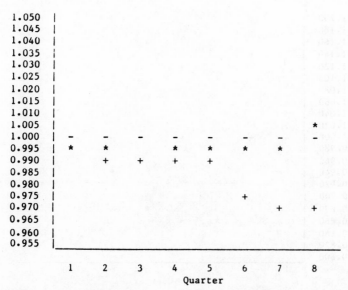

Figure 8.10. Compensation of Employees, Ratio of Two-Year Predictions to Actual (1977–78 = +; 1980–81 = *)

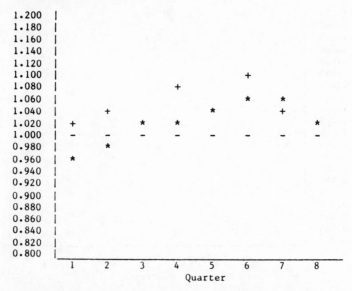

Figure 8.11. Unemployment Rate, Ratio of Quarter Predictions to Actual (1977–78 = +; 1980–81 = ∗)

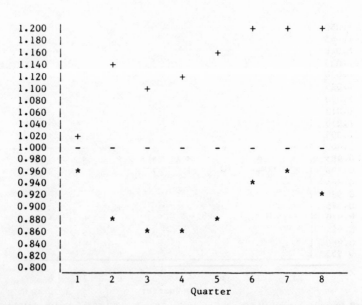

Figure 8.12. Unemployment Rate, Ratio of Two-Year Predictions to Actual (1977–78 = +; 1980–81 = ∗)

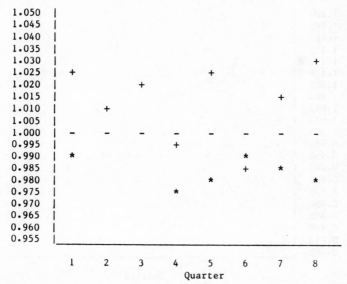

Figure 8.13. Personal Consumption Expenditures, Ratio of Quarter Predictions to Actual (1977–78 = +; 1980–81 = ∗)

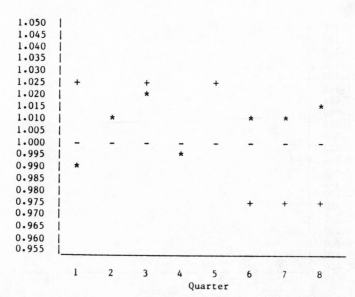

Figure 8.14. Personal Consumption Expenditures, Ratio of Two-Year Predictions to Actual (1977–78 = +; 1980–81 = ∗)

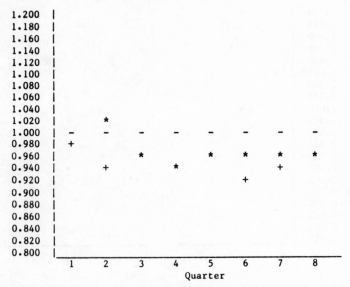

Figure 8.15. Fixed Investment, Ratio of Quarter Predictions to Actual (1977–78 = +; 1980–81 = *)

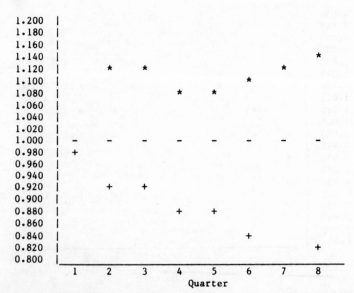

Figure 8.16. Fixed Investment, Ratio of Two-Year Predictions to Actual (1977–78 = +; 1980–81 = *)

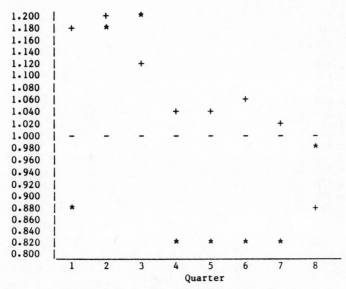

Figure 8.17.   Treasury Bill Rate, Ratio of Quarter Predictions to Actual (1977–78 = +; 1980–81 = ∗)

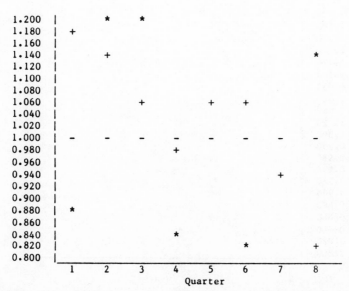

Figure 8.18.   Treasury Bill Rate, Ratio of Two-Year Predictions to Actual (1977–78 = +; 1980–81 = ∗)

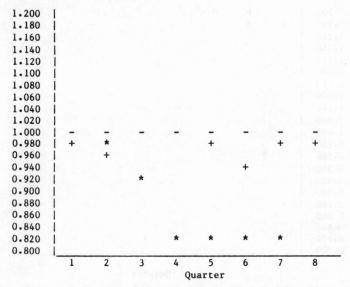

Figure 8.19. Treasury Bond Rate, Ratio of Quarter Predictions to Actual (1977–78 = +; 1980–81 = *)

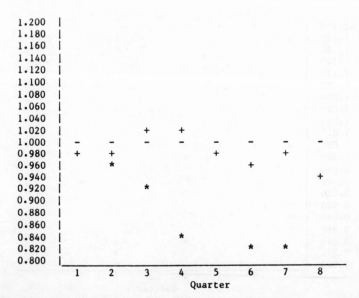

Figure 8.20. Treasury Bond Rate, Ratio of Two-Year Predictions to Actual (1977–78 = +; 1980–81 = *)

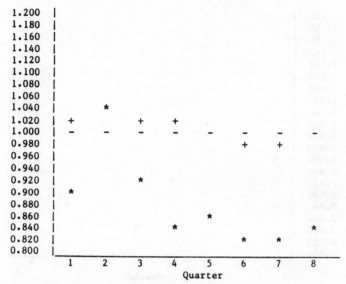

Figure 8.21.   Mortgage Rate, Ratio of Quarter Predictions to Actual (1977–78 = +; 1980–81 = ∗)

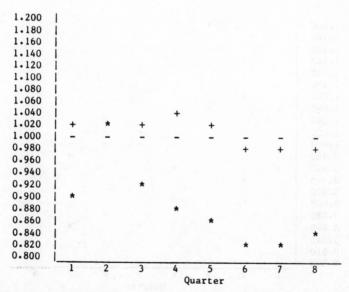

Figure 8.22.   Mortgage Rate, Ratio of Two-Year Predictions to Actual (1977–78 = +; 1980–81 = ∗)

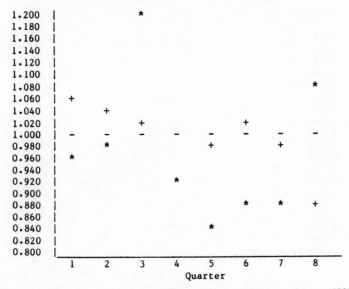

Figure 8.23. Bank Loan Rate, Ratio of Quarter Predictions to Actual (1977–78 = +; 1980–81 = *)

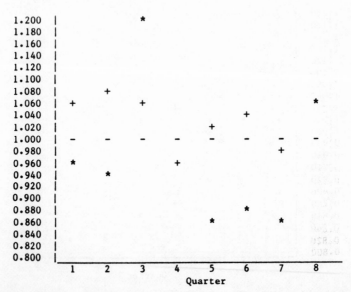

Figure 8.24. Bank Loan Rate, Ratio of Two-Year Predictions to Actual (1977–78 = +; 1980–81 = *)

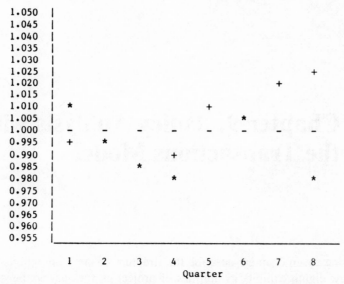

Figure 8.25. Money Supply (M2), Ratio of Quarter Predictions to Actual (1977–78 = +; 1980–81 = *)

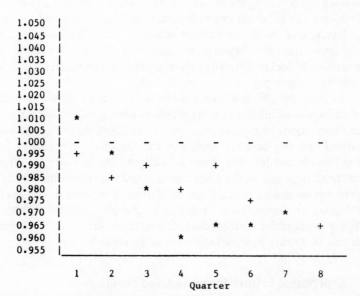

Figure 8.26. Money Supply (M2), Ratio of Two-Year Predictions to Actual (1977–78 = +; 1980–81 = *)

Chapter 9. Policy Analysis with the Transactions Model

The first seven chapters describe the structure of the Transactions Model and the eighth exhibits its abilities of projection for quarters beyond the period whose data established parameter values. In this chapter, we demonstrate the use of the model to study government policy by performing two experiments.

In the first experiment, we allow the federal government to introduce an indexed bond, and then we record its effects on other interest rates and on the federal debt service. In the second experiment, we reduce the standard workweek (by requiring the payment of overtime for fewer than forty hours) and observe the effect on unemployment, productivity, profits, wage and price levels, and the distribution of income.[1] The experiments are intrinsically interesting. But they also demonstrate both the ease with which the Transactions Model realistically delineates policies and the ease with which the effects of these policies may be studied.

To study the effects of indexed bonds, the model allows us to specify the distribution of inflationary expectations among individual actors, how these expectations change as time passes, and how these expectations are translated into buy and sell orders to the financial intermediary for the indexed bonds and for other financial obligations. To study the effects of hours' reduction, the model takes into account the short-run fixed proportions of capital and labor and treats with some semblance of realism firms' adjustments to changing cost schedules, changing supply of labor, and changing demand for their product. It also treats the issue of the pro-rata reduction in weekly pay, including fringe benefits.

Experiment I: Introducing Indexed Bonds

The benefits of the issuance by the federal government of bonds indexed to inflation have been dealt with by a number of authors (Fischer 1975, 1979;

Weiner 1983). Their most obvious direct effect is, of course, in allaying people's anxiety that inflation will erode their assets. A second direct effect is that the issuer assumes different liabilities from those it would have assumed by issuing conventional securities.

To experiment with the effects of indexed bonds, we must specify the nature of the bond, the strategy of the issuer, the formation of people's inflation expectations, and the portfolio behavior of households and firms in the face of these expectations. (Portfolio decisions by each of these firms are made by a group of the model's individuals, controlling equal shares of the firm's portfolio and behaving on the firm's behalf with respect to the bonds as they behave on their own behalf.) In specifying all of these things, we must obviously make somewhat arbitrary choices. The degree of arbitrariness is perhaps reduced by simulating with alternative sets of specifications. This, however, throws back to the reader the task of deciding which specifications are most realistic, at least when the outcomes are sensitive to the specifications.

Bond Specification

We specify an indexed bond with the following characteristics: it is a perpetuity; its value is fully indexed to the consumer price index; and the federal government redeems all units presented to it at any time for a price in dollars equal to the CPI ruling at that time. In this sense, from the point of view of those who hold them, indexed bonds are similar to a unit of currency backed by a commodity bundle, whose price moves with the CPI. The indexed bond does not pay interest, aside from its growth in dollar value with inflation. As with all other government debt instruments, all trading is done through the financial intermediary, which sets a price in accordance with supply and demand. The price depends, of course, on people's inflation expectations and on the amount of these bonds in the public's hands, an amount partially controlled by the government.

Given the above specifications, the bond can trade at a price over the CPI. It does not, however, trade at a discount, because the alternative of redemption at the CPI precludes that. The tax treatment of the increase in the value of the indexed bond must also be specified. We chose to treat the increase like ordinary interest and thus subject to taxation at regular rates.

Issuance Strategy

Given inflation expectations and redemption provisions, there is an upper limit to the stock of indexed bonds the public wants to hold at any time. If a change in the balance between supply and demand should drop the price that would clear the market below the CPI, the financial intermediary would present indexed bonds to the treasury for redemption until the price rose to the level of the CPI.

Within that constraint, however, the government has discretion as to the stock it maintains. The maximum stock varies through time, depending on inflation expectations and on interest rates on alternative assets. (These alternative interest rates may themselves be affected by the issuance of the indexed bond; this is one of the factors explored in the experiment.) If the government maintains a low stock, a small quantity can be sold at a high price to those people with the most extreme inflationary expectations. A large stock requires lower prices to float.

Maintaining the maximum quantity at a zero premium best serves the purpose of providing relief to the public from inflation anxieties. (Of course, selling these bonds with fixed redemption dates at a discount might serve that purpose even better; however, we ruled that out in the interest of simplicity.) On the other hand, lowering the stock below the minimum size lowers the interest burden of the public debt—but at the expense of those households and firms with the highest expectation of inflation. In effect, the government sells them inflation insurance at a high price and uses the proceeds to lower the burden on the other taxpayers. Another factor that bears on the strategy of the government is the effect of the indexed bonds on other financial markets. In the simulation, some runs assume a strategy of maximal issue and others a strategy of restricted issue.

Demand for the Bonds

In our descriptions of behavior in earlier chapters, we do not specify the formation of expectations of inflation. In this application of the model, such a specification is obviously necessary.

Each person represented in the model forms an expectation of the rate of inflation over the medium-term future. This expectation, continually updated, is based on the current rate of inflation and recent changes in the rate of inflation. The average person expects that the increase in prices will be

$$\text{PEXP} = [[\text{P(T)}/\text{P(T} - 12)]**4] - 1 \tag{9.1}$$
$$+ \text{ACC}*[\text{P(T)}/\text{P(T} - 12) - \text{P(T} - 12)/\text{P(T} - 24)].$$

Thus, on average, people expect that the rate of inflation over the next year will be the annualized rate of inflation experienced over the last quarter, with an add-on for the acceleration in the inflation rate for the last quarter over the quarter previous to that. The parameter ACC governs the weight given to the acceleration factor. The simulation is run with ACC at 0.5 or 1.0.

While equation 9.1 controls the mean rate of inflation expected, people's expectations are assumed to be normally distributed around the mean.

The ratio of the standard deviation to the mean, SIGEXP, was set at 0.5 for some runs and 0.25 for others, allowing us to assess the difference made by both low clustering and high clustering. While this configuration gives appreciable numbers of people with negative inflation expectations even in times of high inflation, it is only people with relatively high positive expectations who consider buying the indexed bonds.

The *J*th actor in the model is assumed to consider unloading conventional assets and replacing them by indexed bonds when

$$\text{DIFF} = [\text{EXPINF(J)}/(1 + \text{PREM}) - \text{R}]/\text{R} > 0. \tag{9.2}$$

EXPINF(J) is the Jth individual's expectation of the rate of inflation; R is the current average rate of return on the noncash assets in the individual's portfolio; and PREM is the rate of premium in the market price of the indexed bond.

Each household or firm that considers the indexed bonds to be good investments must decide how many to buy. Those whose expectations of inflation are such that they are on the margin of doubt as to whether the indexed bonds are a good investment buy none of them. Those with expectations of higher rates of inflation convert a proportion of their noncash, nonequity assets to indexed bonds according to

$$\text{Proportion converted} = \text{CONV}*\text{DIFF}. \tag{9.3}$$

DIFF is the quantity defined in equation 9.2, and CONV is a behavioral parameter. When CONV is one, a household or firm is assumed to convert 100 percent of its eligible assets to indexed bonds when the expected return on them reaches or exceeds twice the return on conventional assets. In the simulations, CONV has the values one and two.

Economic Results of the Issuance

The simulation results suggest that in periods of inflation the federal government can achieve important current budgetary savings through the introduction of a zero-coupon indexed bond with a redemption value hitched to the consumer price index. However, the reduction of regular interest payments by the government has a depressing effect, and the effect on financial markets for conventional obligations is considerable.

The results under various assumptions about public reactions to the bonds are presented in table 9.1. Under standard assumptions (1) PREM, the percentage by which the market price of the indexed bonds exceeds the consumer price index, is maintained at zero by the federal government as a matter of policy. The government controls this magnitude through its ability to increase or decrease the issue of indexed bonds. (2) SIGEXP, the ratio of the standard deviation to the mean value of inflation expectations, is 0.5. (3)

Table 9.1. Effects of introducing indexed bonds under various assumptions (billions of dollars)

	1977–78			1980–81		
Assumption	Average Outstanding	Federal Interest Change	Federal Deficit Change	Average Outstanding	Federal Interest Change	Federal Deficit Change
Standard*a*	143.5	−17.7	−8.6	446.0	−55.6	−37.6
PREM = 0.02						
or higher	116.4	−21.6	−9.6	409.9	−57.2	−39.4
PREM = 0.05						
or higher	88.7	−31.9	−14.2	391.2	58.4	−35.3
SIGEXP = 0.25	76.0	−15.1	−6.9	438.8	−52.5	−35.8
ACC = 1.00	146.6	−17.9	−6.2	375.1	−43.7	−29.5
CONV = 2.00	211.4	−26.7	−14.9	643.2	−83.4	−60.5

NOTE: PREM is the fraction of the purchase price charged by the government as a premium for the inflation insurance provided by the indexed bond. SIGEXP is the ratio of the standard deviation to the mean for inflation expectations. ACC is the weight of the relative change in the consumer price index between the two previous quarters in forming inflation expections. CONV is an index of the importance households attach to the excess of the expected return on indexed bonds over the average return on the current portfolio.
*a*Standard assumptions are PREM = 0.0 or higher; SIGEXP = 0.5; ACC = 0.5; and CONV = 1.0.

ACC, the acceleration factor in inflation expectations, is 0.5. That is, people form their inflation expectations by adding half of the relative change in the CPI between the two previous quarters to the current quarter's change in the CPI. (4) CONV, the constant that controls the fraction of eligible assets converted to indexed bonds, is assumed to be one.

The results using this standard set of assumptions are presented in the first line of table 9.1. If indexed bonds were introduced at the beginning of 1977, the public would hold $143.5 billion of them over the next two years. An introduction at the beginning of 1980 results in holdings over the 1980–81 period of $446.0 billion. The major difference in the two periods is, of course, that the inflation rate is twice as high in the second period. Some interest rates are also twice as high in the second period—or even higher. However, interest rates on savings accounts and bonds are low relative to the rate of inflation at the start of the second period, and this causes households and firms to buy large quantities of the indexed bonds. As explained below, the subsequent movement of these interest rates does not reverse the flow into indexed bonds.

Household holdings of indexed bonds in the two periods are $133.1 and $300.8 billion, respectively. Households are programmed to compare the expected return on these bonds with the average return on their savings accounts, treasury bills, treasury bonds, municipal bonds, and private bonds. However, only about 10 percent of the households hold securities other than savings accounts, so for most of the households the comparison is between the expected return on the indexed bonds and the current return on savings accounts. Nonfinancial firms hold no savings accounts; however, in the second period, interest rates on conventional bonds are low enough for them also to acquire large quantities of indexed bonds.

Government Budget Effects.   Under the standard assumptions, the federal government reduces its interest payments by $55.6 billion over the second period. The net reduction in the federal deficit is somewhat lower, at $37.6 billion, because the experiment reduced the level of economic activity compared with historic levels and consequently reduced tax collections.

The second and third lines of table 9.1 show that the government makes a somewhat higher profit—in terms of reducing the interest charge—if it restricts the supply of indexed bonds so that they sell at a premium. Limiting the quantity also has the welcome effect of reducing the inflation-swollen amounts that get reconverted to regular debt when inflation eases and the indexed bonds are turned in to the treasury.

However, the major benefit to the government derives from selling the indexed bonds at a premium when large amounts of conventional bonds are converted. This happens at the time of their initial introduction, when the premium can be collected on that portion of the stock of previously accumulated debt converted to indexed form. It might also happen when expectations of inflation increase sharply. At other times, the premium can be collected only on a part of the new debt.

Macroeconomic Effects.   Why does the issuance of indexed bonds reduce economic activity? Purchasers of the indexed bonds are required to pay the same rate of taxes on the appreciation in the value of their indexed bonds as they would pay on interest received on alternative assets. For the alternative assets, they receive the interest as a cash flow, whereas for indexed bonds the return is only a paper profit, which must be held to preserve the real value of the asset. Thus, holders of indexed bonds have a reduced flow to consume and to purchase homes, resulting in a reduction of consumer expenditures of $6.4 billion per year.

The resultant fall in aggregate demand reduces indirect business-tax receipts of the federal government by $0.6 billion per year. The reduced demand for consumer goods also reduces labor demand, raising the unemployment rate an average of 0.2 percentage points and reducing compensation of employees by an average of $4.1 billion per year. The result is a lowering in personal income-tax liabilities for wage income, offset however by higher tax liabilities on indexed-bond paper profits, because these exceed the returns on alternative assets. The higher unemployment results in an estimated average of $0.6 billion more per year in government transfer payments. The lower level of economic activity also reduces corporate profits by $25.5 billion per year, which reduces federal tax collections on corporate profits by $7.1 billion per year.

Effects on Financial Markets and Institutions.   The financial impacts of the indexed bonds are worth noting. As indexed bonds are issued, the federal government must retire conventional securities in quantities consistent with the need to finance the current deficit in its cash flow; it retires a uniform fraction of all types and maturities of conventional bonds. The financial institutions, the governments, the monetary authority, and the rest-of-world cannot purchase indexed bonds; thus they continue to demand conventional government securities in quantities altered only by changes in interest rates precipitated by introduction of the indexed bonds.

The households and nonfinancial firms historically hold only 30 percent of the outstanding treasury bills. However, they purchase 100 percent of the indexed bonds. As the treasury retires treasury bills to issue indexed bonds, an excess demands for bills arises—thus the bill rate falls an average of 0.8 percentage points over the two years. The parameter that controls the speed of adjustment of the bill rate to excess demand was estimated over the 1967–78 period—a period during which excess demands and supplies were far smaller than the excess demand resulting from introducing indexed bonds. Thus an excess demand approximating $60 billion on average persists during the 1980–81 period and is satisfied by the financial intermediary with short sales of bills. The same process is true to a lesser extent for treasury bonds. (Whether in reality the addiction to treasury bills would be so extreme on the part of financial institutions is somewhat beyond the scope of our research effort. Nevertheless, the simulation does point up interesting ramifications of the change in availability of debt instruments.)

The Transactions Model's output includes a balance sheet for the bank, and this provides a handy way of gauging the effects of the issuance of indexed bonds on the financial side of the economy. The bank's end-of-1981 balance sheet shows that (1) money liabilities decline $44 billion, (2) savings accounts decline $68 billion, (3) other liabilities decline $38 billion, (4) consumer loans decline $4 billion, (5) business loans decline $103 billion, (6) bill holdings remain largely unchanged, (7) bond holdings decline $40 billion, and (8) mortgage holdings decline $30 billion.

The financial intermediary (which makes the market in the new indexed bonds, bills, other bonds, and mortgages) experiences substantial declines in its liabilities and increases in its cash as it meets demand for bills and bonds while unable to use the proceeds of the sale to purchase earning assets. Thus the effects on the financial intermediary's end-of-1981 portfolio are (1) a decrease of $110 billion in its bank-loan liabilities, (2) an increase of $34 billion in its holdings of mortgages (largely because bank demand for them declines), (3) a decline of $62 billion in its holdings of bills (almost entirely because of the federal government's reducing issuance as it sells indexed bonds), and (4) a decline of $59 billion in its holdings of bonds of all types other than indexed (because of federal government retirements).

Sensitivity of Results to Assumptions on Portfolio Behavior

The last three lines of table 9.1 show the sensitivity of the results to the assumptions about portfolio behavior in response to the issuance of indexed bonds. As might be expected, the results are quite sensitive to the assumption concerning the proportion of assets households and firms wish to convert to indexed form. There appears, however, to be relatively little sensitivity to size of the acceleration parameter, or to the size of the standard deviation of expectations in the population.

Experiment II: Reducing Hours of Work

The second experiment was on the effects of a policy designed to reduce unemployment by reducing standard hours in the workweek. Unemployment rates have had a generally upward trend in the United States since 1969. Rates in each successive recovery failed to reach the lows they achieved in the previous recovery.

The unfavorable unemployment trend is probably due to a number of causes, rather than any one. Intensifying inflation, due in part to Vietnam-era fiscal strains and in part to shocks from oil and agricultural prices, occasioned restrictive monetary policies, which exacerbated the unemployment problem by depressing demand for goods and services. The rapid growth of women's participation in the labor force and a flood of illegal immigrants have put a strain on the capacity of the economy to absorb new workers. Productivity, although advancing at a low rate in recent years, has about doubled since the end of World War II.

The standard legal workweek, beyond which overtime pay is compulsory, has remained fixed for more than four decades. Average hours have fallen somewhat, as the proportion of people on part-time schedules has increased, but for the majority of workers on full-time schedules, no lowering of hours has occurred. In the past, reducing standard hours of work and increasing the amount of leisure and of work around the home has been a way to "spend" some of the increase in productivity.

In the American economy, employers can be expected to resist government action that would make them pay premium overtime rates after a lower number of hours. Establishment-by-establishment changes in workweek are also hard to make; if an establishment replaces an advance in weekly pay with a cut in standard hours, it might lose its more work-prone employees to establishments that do the opposite.

Another factor slowing cuts in weekly hours is fringe benefits figured on a per-worker rather than a per-hour basis. Health insurance is the most obvious example. If total compensation is cut proportionately to hours but health benefits remain unchanged, workers' cash wage will fall more than their hours. The favorable tax treatment accorded these benefits reduces flexibility in dealing with them.

Whether or not the fixity of the standard workweek has increased unemployment, a reduced workweek may well decrease it. The simulation is designed to estimate the effects on unemployment and other variables of a reduced workweek.

Specification of the Experiment

In the Transactions Model, weekly hours determine the output obtained from the combination of a week's work of one worker with a machine of a particular vintage. Reducing weekly hours while keeping output fixed involves activating older and therefore less productive vintages of capital equipment, at least in the short run. The actual effect of a reduction of hours on output is, of course, something to be determined endogenously, as output is affected by changes in demand as well as changes in productivity.

Firms in the model maintain a constant "standard" workweek peculiar to their industry. However, hours per week actually worked depends on responses to changes in demand. Employers expand weekly work hours of production workers as a short-run response to the need for an increase in production occasioned by a rise in demand for the product. When the workweek is higher than the standard, employers make gradual reductions in the workweek until it reaches the standard and hire more workers so as to maintain output (see equation 4.8). Reductions in output are treated symmetrically.

The simulated reduction in standard hours for production workers is accomplished by reducing that level of their weekly hours to which firms try to gravitate when the level of demand is steady. The number of production workers employed is a variable determined endogenously and is influenced by changes in demand as well as changes in hours. However, the employment of nonproduction workers requires different treatment. Employers are assumed to want to maintain intact the number of person-hours worked by the fixed staff. They therefore increase this staff in proportion to the cut in hours for variable staff.

The treatment of pay is crucial to the outcome of the simulation. If weekly pay for a standard workweek is kept the same while standard hours are cut, then sizable increases in unit cost will occur, and there will be upward pressures on prices. If weekly pay is cut proportionately with the hours' reduction, then proportional increases in costs are avoided. However, some unit-cost increases result if output fails to drop. The reason for this is that, as noted above, the firm has to use older capital vintages.

(Some industries, particularly trade and banking, maintain considerable numbers of part-time workers. The Transactions Model does not distinguish between full-time and part-time workers and attributes to each worker in a firm the same weekly hours, namely, an appropriately weighted average of full-time hours and part-time hours. If the standard workweek for full-time workers is reduced, part-time workers might want to avoid a reduction in their weekly hours. If employers accede, average hours actually worked would not drop to the same extent.)

In the simulation, we ignore the finer points of issues like fringe benefits and part timers. When standard hours are reduced, we reduce hours for all workers, and we reduce weekly compensation (which includes fringe benefits) proportionately for all workers.

As in the case of the indexed bond, simulations were run for two historical periods of two years each. For each period, two runs of the model were made, one reducing the standard hours by 2 percent and one by 5 percent. These reductions amount to about ten minutes per day and twenty-five minutes per day, respectively, in a five-day workweek.

Results

The numerical results of the simulation are shown in table 9.2. Reductions in hours reduce the unemployment rate substantially although slightly less than proportionately. For the 1980–81 period, a reduction of 5 percent in the weekly hours results in a four-point drop in the unemployment rate, equivalent to a 4.2-percent rise in the employment rate. What this means is that

Table 9.2. Effects of reducing standard workweek

Variable	1977–78		1980–81	
	2 percent Reduction	5 percent Reduction	2 percent Reduction	5 percent Reduction
Unemployment rate (percentage points)	−0.08	−3.2	−1.6	−4.0
GNP price deflator (percentage points)	0.00	1.5	0.1	0.6
Gross national product (billions of dollars)	−4.20	−11.3	−12.4	−25.7
Compensation of emloyees (billions of dollars)	−6.10	−6.7	−0.9	−3.4
Personal income (billions of dollars)	−8.10	−16.3	−13.1	−25.7
Corporate profits (billions of dollars)	1.70	−2.5	−5.5	−10.7
Federal transfer payments (billions of dollars)	−2.70	−8.8	−7.4	−13.9
Federal deficit (billions of dollars)	−2.10	−4.9	−4.0	−4.6
Gini coefficient change (percent)	0.00	0.0	0.0	−2.0

the drop in aggregate demand due to the fall in the average weekly wage is almost but not quite offset by the rise in the number of workers employed. The cut of 5 percent in weekly hours causes a reduction of 1 percent in real GNP over this period.

The 5-percent cut in hours has a modest effect on the distribution of income: the Gini coefficient drops from 0.423 to 0.414. The drop in hours also presumably increases well-being through increasing leisure. The effect on personal income averages −$25.7 billion, a fall of 1.1 percent. Aggregate payrolls fall even though more people are working. A fall in transfer payments for unemployment insurance of $13.9 billion also contributes to the fall in personal income.

While the slightly reduced rate of taxable economic activity cuts tax collections, this is more than offset by the fall in transfer payments. The government deficit drops as a result.

Given the vintage capital structure of the Transactions Model and the assumption that output is at all times being produced on the vintages that yield the highest labor productivity, the fall in hours with no short-run change in machinery available causes a drop in productivity. Less productive, older machines previously serving as spare capacity are pressed into service as new workers are hired. This fall in the productivity of production workers causes a rise in unit labor costs, which causes some extra inflation. However, the magnitude of this effect is a mere 0.6 percent in the GNP deflator over the 1980–81 period. For the earlier period, this effect is 1.5 percent.

In the longer run, the reduction in hours and the resultant extention of production to older and less-productive vintages of capital equipment should spark extra investment, as firms have more incentive to replace old machines with new machines. However, this effect is not apparent in the two-year runs, in part because of decreased production.

The Transactions Model and Policy Studies

The two policy studies reported in this chapter are exemplars of the virtues and weaknesses of the Transactions Model in its present state of development. The chief weaknesses are that results depend on many assumptions, some of them having little to recommend them over other assumptions, and that the methodology for estimating parameters needs developing.

The chief virtue of the model is that policies can be represented realistically. A second virtue, less obvious in advance of doing the studies themselves, is that the model facilitates looking for and understanding unforeseen second-order consequences of policies. This is most obvious in the indexed-bond study, where, to us at any rate, the effect on the financial markets was hard to foresee.

We are confident, as a result of our long and quite arduous experience with the Transactions Model, that as time passes the virtues of this methodology will be further developed and the defects further reduced by hands more apt for the work than ours.

Appendix. Parameter estimates for equations in Chapters 4, 5, and 6

Equation Number and Type	Parameter Value				AAPE	$\bar{R}^2$
	$a(1)$	$a(2)$	$a(3)$	$a(4)$		
4.1,A						
4.2,R	1.923	−6.461	0.00101		1.37	.658
	(196.5)	(−4.29)	(7.97)			
4.3,A						
4.4,R	0.0195				0.35	.751
	(1624.)					
4.5,E	0.2					
4.6,A						
4.7,A						
4.8,I	0.0909					
4.9,I						
Firm 1	0.00003					
Firm 2	0.00076					
Firm 3	−0.0006					
Firm 4	−0.0008					
Firm 5	−0.0004					
Firm 6	−0.0003					
Firm 7	−0.0005					
Firm 8	−0.0001					
Firm 9	−0.0005					
Firm 10	0.00034					
Firm 11	−0.0009					
Firm 12	−0.0012					
4.10,A						
4.11,A						
4.12,R	(Available on request)					
4.13,E	(Available on request)					
4.14,E	0.990					
4.15,A						

(continued)

Appendix (*continued*)

Equation Number and Type	Parameter Value				AAPE	$\bar{R}^2$
	$a(1)$	$a(2)$	$a(3)$	$a(4)$		
4.16,E	0.044					
4.17,A						
4.18,R	−0.00977	0.01287	0.01092		58.9	.664
	(−4.070)	(7.142)	(4.535)			
4.19,A						
4.20,A						
4.21,A						
4.22,A						
4.23,A						
4.24,A						
4.25,A						
4.26,A						
4.27,R	0.02367	0.9654			1.18	.998
	(6.164)	(80.26)				
4.28,E						
4.29,A						
4.30,A						
4.31,I						
Firm 1	0.00229					
Firm 2	0.0027					
Firm 3	−0.0007					
Firm 4	0.00006					
Firm 5	0.00038					
Firm 6	0.00117					
Firm 7	0.00296					
Firm 8	0.00139					
Firm 9	0.00170					
Firm 10	0.00151					
Firm 11	0.00085					
Firm 12	−0.0008					
4.32,I						
Firm 1	−0.0177					
Firm 2	0.00747					
Firm 3	−0.00245					
Firm 4	−0.01475					
Firm 5	−0.01178					
Firm 6	−0.01765					
Firm 7	−0.02467					
Firm 8	0.001649					
Firm 9	−0.00123					
Firm 10	0.005014					
Firm 11	−0.02111					
Firm 12	−0.01367					
4.33,A						
4.34,A						
4.35,I						
4.36,E	0.1438					

Appendix (*continued*)

Equation Number and Type	Parameter Value a(1)	a(2)	a(3)	a(4)	AAPE	$\bar{R}^2$
4.37,I						
Firm 1	0.0788					
Firm 2	0.0611					
Firm 3	0.2827					
Firm 4	0.6316					
Firm 5	0.1683					
Firm 6	0.1471					
Firm 7	0.2743					
Firm 8	0.5217					
Firm 9	0.5847					
Firm 10	0.0639					
Firm 11	0.3908					
Firm 12	0.8500					
4.38,E	1.044					
4.39,A						
4.40,E	0.4356					
4.41,R	3.519 (59.99)	−2.384 (−4.052)	−0.00062 (−5.642)		3.20	.679
5.1,R	3790. (23.41)	0.186 (9.339)	5.803 (0.1745)	10.76 (11.45)	0.20	.998
5.2,R	−28960. (−17.19)	0.7095 (33.92)	68.58 (3.646)	−5.02 (−4.837)	0.22	.999
5.3,A						
5.4,R	0.1214 (18.62)	−0.0013 (−1.156)			9.08	.001
5.5,E	0.25					
5.6,R	0.03082 (3.70)	0.03306 (16.57)	−0.00013 (−3.25)		6.31	.855
5.7,A						
5.8,A						
5.9,A						
5.10,A						
5.11,A						
5.12,E						
5.13,E						
5.14,I	2.705	0.2092				
5.15,R	0.08713 (195.9)				3.60	.988
5.16,A						
5.17,I	(*See table 5.1*)					
5.18,I	0.925	0.2245				
5.19,I	(*See table 5.1*)					
5.20,I	0.005584					
5.21,I	1.000					
5.22,A						
5.23,A						
5.24,I	0.1612					

(*continued*)

Appendix (*continued*)

Equation Number and Type	Parameter Value a(1)	a(2)	a(3)	a(4)	AAPE	$\bar{R}^2$
5.25,A						
5.26,R	(*See table 5.2*)					
6.1,R	0.0688 (19.09)	−0.3568 (−2.74)	0.00017 (21.62)		7.51	.903
6.2,A						
6.3,R	0.0556 (1.905)	1.232 (4.344)	−4.837 (−2.890)	−0.00015 (−3.507)	148.04	.300
6.4,R	0.01455 (7.191)	−0.0804 (−2.559)			33.16	.098
6.5,R	(*See table 6.2*)					
6.6,R	−0.0197	2.267	0.0010		6.33	.924
6.7,R	0.0969 (48.95)	0.0890 (5.203)	0.0010		2.58	.338
6.8,R	0.04396 (57.23)	0.08212 (5.720)	0.000034 (29.41)		1.65	.966
6.9,R	0.1109 (82.03)	−0.0695 (−2.501)	0.000056 (16.21)		2.79	.856
6.10,R	37.40 (6.42)	−343.3 (−2.965)	0.01633 (2.714)		13.33	.119
6.11,R	(*See table 6.3*)					
6.12,R	−0.0727 (−5.396)	0.5782 (9.300)	0.000182 (8.557)	0.0010	10.13	.838
6.13,R	0.02846 (18.42)	0.3107 (10.76)	0.000033 (14.26)	0.0010	3.55	.925
6.14,R	0.04387 (21.94)	0.5449 (14.58)	0.000032 (10.90)	0.0010	3.05	.928

NOTE: Types of equations are: A—accounting identities; or parameters are filled by; R—linear regression; I—an iterative process; E—through extraneous estimation. AAPE is average absolute percentage error; t-statistics are in parentheses.

Notes

Chapter 1. Introduction

1. See Arrow (1951). Our treatment of expectations is more thorough in the indexed-bond experiment in chapter 9.

Chapter 2. Framework of the Transactions Model

1. When in the course of a run of the model, people leave the labor force, they continue to be represented as individuals, and their assets and/or liabilities remain with them.

2. Flow inputs, following the input-output tradition, are not price elastic.

Chapter 4. The Firms

1. So that the text can serve as a guide to the FORTRAN program of the model, we have attempted to make the equations in the text conform to the greatest extent possible to the program. Thus, there are some magnitudes, such as total cost (TCOST) that are obviously different for different firms but that have not been given firm-specific subscripts because they do not have them in the program.

2. The production setup of the firm and the specification of the change in the productiveness of new capital equipment are similar to the system described by Salter (1960) and Solow et al. (1966).

3. Firms and sectors with no inventories are capital-intensive services, other services, financial intermediaries, bank, the federal government, and state/local government. The product of wholesale and retail trade is a service, but since that product is only demanded in association with the goods of other firms as a markup, we treat its product as a good. The construction firm, although its final product is structures, is represented as maintaining no inventories of finished goods. This follows the procedures of the

national accounts. Structures are converted from goods in process into finished goods in the round after they are paid for—approximately thirty rounds after their production is initiated. The import industry's inventories of its own products are not represented, although the model's firms are assumed to hold inventories of the import industry's product.

4. This equation is estimated at the aggregate level over the 1967–79 period, with a moving average of a total-sales analog of the national accounts inventory/sales ratio as the dependent variable. The average weekly change in the relevant GNP deflator over the previous quarter is the independent variable. Despite the $\bar{R}^2$ of .66, this equation results in an average absolute percentage error of only 1.37 for this adjusted ratio of inventory to sales over the 1967–79 period.

5. Estimation of the speed-of-adjustment parameter was started by running the model using a trial value. For a round, the discrepancy, ERR, between the endogenously computed inventory change and that indicated by national accounts of the 1967–79 period was calculated. At the end of the round, orders and inventory change were reset to reflect the actual inventory change shown by the national accounts. This procedure produces an average aggregate inventory-change discrepancy, ERR, for each run. We obtain a new trial value of the parameter $a(1)$ from

$$a(1) = a(1)_o * \frac{\overline{DINVC} - \overline{PINVC} + \overline{ERR}}{\overline{DINVC} - \overline{PINVC}},$$

and continue until the change in the parameter value between runs is less than 1 percent.

6. See Fair (1969) and Ehrenberg (1971). Brechling 1965 uses a model in which hours are adjusted in the short run, while employment changes occur in the long run.

7. Fitted by an interative procedure to cross-industry monthly data. See note 5 for another example of this methodology.

8. An iterative procedure was used to estimate the a(IFIRM). For disembodied technical change, see Denison (1962). For a few firms, a unit of new capital produces less output than the previous vintage. These are, of course, particularly labor saving.

9. The parameters a(IFIRM) and b(IFIRM) are derived by fitting equations of the form

$$E(ijt) = a(ij) + b(ij)\,T + c(ij)\,X + d(ij)\,XT,$$

where $E(ijt)$ is the ith firm's employment of caste j in period t, and X is output. Data on occupations from the Current Population Survey were combined with data on unemployment by industry from the Bureau of Labor Statistics establishment data.

10. The divisions of the total demand for variable labor into demands by occupation are derived from time trends computed on CPS data of employment by occupation.

11. Firms enter the labor market to make hires sequentially. In the case where constraints (4.14) are not met, all firms are required to lower their hiring goals so as to avoid having the entire burden of the short labor supply fall on the firms that enter the labor market last.

12. See Evans (1969), p. 272. The parameter limiting the range of the ratio of actual to standard hours was set at the highest value observed in the data for any of the industry groups in the 1967–79 period.

13. The standard reference in this area continues to be Lintner (1956). Kuh (1963) presents empirical estimates of dividend equations following Lintner's formulation.

14. The fraction of profits distributed by noncorporate firms was fitted tentatively to allow firms' assets to track the flow-of-funds data.

15. If we had programmed the firm to act as economic theorists say profit-maximizing firms do, the firm would first compute its marginal-cost curve (which it can do easily by equation 4.25). It would then estimate its marginal-revenue curve, presumably by reference to its previous experience with changes in demand produced by changes in price. It would then change its price so as to bring marginal revenue and marginal cost closer. However, as each industry is represented by only one firm in the model, we would have had to determine how a U.S. firm's marginal-revenue curve differed from its industry's marginal-revenue curve. The representation we have given of the firm's pricing behavior, which has a cost-plus pricing procedure as its major ingredient, has the virtue of allowing us to sidestep this issue. Whether it has the additional and more important virtue of fidelity to reality is, of course, an empirical question. For a review of the empirical evidence for cost-plus pricing, see Eichner (1973). Hall and Hitch (1939) conducted the original research in this area. See also Cyert and March (1965).

16. If the prescribed increase in one round does not restore the customary profit margin, there will be a price increase in the next round, even if costs have not changed.

17. The tie-in of price behavior and inventory accumulation is discussed by Cyert and March (1965), chaps. 7 and 8. The maximum rate of excess inventory observed in the 1967–79 period was 5 percent.

18. The fraction has the value 0.91 and was computed as the minimum ratio of SALE(IFIRM) to AVSALE(IFIRM) for the 1967–79 period.

19. The unused machine continues to be available for production for outputs higher than those anticipated at the time of the investment decision.

20. An iterative procedure was used to estimate the divisor 336.7, which is the number of rounds a capital good can be operated before being fully depreciated. For the real-estate firm, this parameter is given the value 782.5.

21. The parameter $a(1)$ is the average ratio of Moody's average yield on private bonds to the Federal Reserve Board's market yield on long-term government bonds for the 1967–79 period.

22. The initial values of $a(\text{IFIRM})$ were calculated by taking the mean value for the 1974–79 period of the left-hand-side of the inequality when investment is set exogenously.

23. The parameter $a(1)$ is taken to be the maximum permitted ratio of actual to normal hours of work for a firm. It is the highest value for any firm for any round during the 1967–79 period.

24. A physical unit of housing is defined in the same way a physical unit of any other product is defined: the amount that could be bought for one dollar in 1972. A dwelling unit, the conventional unit of the housing industry, is a collection of the model's physical units. Families of differing incomes buy collections of units of housing of different sizes.

25. For computational convenience, households take out loans from the bank as they make their purchases; at the close of the round, the bank deals out some of these loans to the trade firm and the financial intermediary. These firms will buy from the bank a share of the new consumer-debt instruments created during the round. The average shares are derived from the flow-of-funds accounts.

26. The proportion of new capital equipment financed by bond issues, $a(1)$, is the

mean value for the 1967–79 period of the ratio of new bond issues to investment-goods deliveries.

27. Open-market securities take the form of shares in the portfolio of government bonds and bills and firms' bonds and equities held by the financial intermediary for its own and others' accounts (see chapter 6).

28. This formulation distinguishes poorly between periods when an asset's return is high compared to the return on competing assets and periods when all assets have high returns. Normalizing the weights into shares does cause the two situations to result in different behavior.

Chapter 5. The Households

1. The model of Orcutt, Caldwell, and Wertheimer (1976) is far more explicit in its representation of out-of-the-labor-force individuals and of the kinds of personal transitions that lead to welfare dependency. In this version of the Transactions Model, this treatment of the welfare population is rather summary.

2. IDIS has a mean of zero; 25 percent of the members of each occupational group have IDIS equal to -1; 50 percent equal to 0; and 25 percent equal to $+1$.

3. The dispersion of workers' wages was chosen to match the wage dispersion found in the data base derived from the Consumer Expenditure Survey.

4. In actuality, workers for the U.S. government and for some state and local governments do not pay social security taxes, but they pay a fraction of their wage to a pension fund. We assume that the amounts are comparable to social security taxes. Part of the revenues collected through equation 5.7 are paid over to the state/local government.

5. Each round, the market value of each home is updated by deducting depreciation on a stright-line basis of 3 percent per year and multiplying the resulting depreciated value by the ratio of current to previous new-home prices.

6. Several simplifying assumptions are embodied in this deduction function. First, we assume that single labor-force members have no dependents, while married labor-force members are in households with 3.5 persons, uniformly. Second, the only explicitly itemized deductions are for property taxes and interest payments. The other deductions permitted by the tax laws are taken care of by adjustments to the POL(I).

7. See note 11, below, for an explanation of the method used to estimate these parameters.

8. This value for proportion of capital gain considered as disposable income was suggested by the magnitude of the coefficient of the asset variable in standard comsumption functions in, for example, Wonnacott (1978). Although a capital gain causes a once-for-all increase in disposable income, some additional consumption may result in later rounds due to the lag in reducing desired consumption when disposable income drops (see equation 5.18).

9. The weight of past expenditures was set by maximizing the $\bar{R}^2$ of equation 5.18, when the parameter for the equilibrium savings ratio for discretionary income is held constant at its previous best estimate. With the lag parameter then fixed, the savings ratio is estimated.

10. For a discussion of some aspects of this system in comparison with some alternatives, and for a brief discussion of computation techniques, see Parks (1969), 642–43.

11. To estimate the a(IFIRM) and b(IFIRM), we used an iterative method that is described in Parks (1969). Aggregate consumer purchases by industry data were converted to a per-capita basis. Trial values of the a(IFIRM) were used to allow an estimate of b(IFIRM). The a's were then reestimated, and so on.

12. See chapter 4 for a description of the process of determining the supply of houses and chapter 6 for the process determining the supply of mortgage money.

13. PAUTO is an average of the prices of the automobile firm and the trade firm, weighted appropriately for the round to reflect the retail markup on automobiles.

14. The parameter relating desired automobile payments to EXP was estimated from the macrodata for the 1967–79 period.

Chapter 6. The Financial Institutions

1. For transactions on the goods and services markets and for employment, the bank includes the monetary authority.

2. Formally speaking, the SLs have been incorporated into the model's bank, but their operations are segregated. Since regulation of their interest rates has affected their performance, and since the future is unlikely to be similar to the past, we have treated much of their activity as exogenous.

3. The numerator of the dependent variable in this equation is the sum of all liabilities of the bank sector and thrift-institution sectors in the flow-of-funds accounts, less their demand, time, and savings-deposit liabilities. It excludes the savings shares of thrift institutions and banks' liabilities to the Federal Reserve. The denominator of the dependent variable is the total financial assets of these sectors.

4. This sale also will result in the financial intermediary's ending the round with a larger inventory of securities, raising their interest rate above what it otherwise would have been.

5. In fitting these equations, the interest rate on a representative single asset might have been a superior choice. Attempts to use the return on the asset less the cost of obtaining the funds gave poor results.

6. In the United States, savings deposits are provided by commercial banks and by specialized savings institutions, and various regulatory authorities have set maximum rates for several different kinds of savings accounts. We have not attempted to represent these complexities in this version of the model.

7. The necessity for short sales of treasury bills arises when the monetary authority fixes the amount of reserves at historical levels without regard to the state of the system and when weak demand for bank loans allows excess reserves to develop, which result in large demands by the bank for treasury bills. Alternative methods of handling this problem are (1) to have interest rates move downward sharply and (2) to have the treasury sell bills for cash in the amount necessary. When the monetary authority is endogenous, it is programmed to sop up excess reserves so as to reduce the bank's demand for bills.

Chapter 7. The Governments and the Monetary Authority

1. The employees of the federal government and of some state and local governments in the United States are not part of the social security system. However, these

workers and the governments that employ them do have more-or-less equivalent retirement funds to which they contribute. This is handled in the model by having all employees pay into the federal social-security fund. When the employer is the federal government, an imputed flow (which affects the national accounts but not the flow-of-funds accounts) for employer social-insurance payments occurs in the proportion POL (13) of the federal government wage bill, set at the rate indicated in the national income accounts. When the employer is the state/local government, it pays for social-insurance purposes an amount equal to the fraction POL(15) of its wage bill to the federal government and an amount equal to the fraction POL(11) into the local government pension fund.

2. In the United States, these home mortgages are owned by quasi-governmental agencies, such as the Government National Mortgage Association.

3. The government sells its bills and bonds to the financial intermediary, which may be able to purchase them for cash. To the extent that the financial intermediary has to resort to bank loans to do so, the effect is merely to shift the bank-loan liabilities from the federal government to the financial intermediary. The financial intermediary cannot float off any of the new government bonds or bills to the bank, the nonfinancial firms, or the households until the next round.

4. All of the governments' cash accounts are deposits at the bank to allow use of the TRANS subroutine for all transactions. In the United States, the federal government's working balances are at the Federal Reserve. Minor adjustments in bank reserves required by this difference are made in the model.

5. If the model's government runs a simulated surplus at a time the United States is running a deficit, there will be a buildup in the cash account of the simulated government. For runs for past periods, this is the only occasion on which the federal government's simulated cash account is allowed to differ from the actual. In such a case, subsequent simulated deficits are financed out of the cash account until the latter is in line with the actual federal cash account as indicated in the flow-of-funds reports.

6. The state/local government brings its holdings of open-market securities, BBONDS(IGOVO), to the level indicated in the flow-of-funds accounts. These securities are primarily those owned by the various retirement funds operated by state and local governments. The simulated state/local government does not issue bills; it issues only new bonds, BONDS(IGOVO,180), in an amount that is sufficient to retire any short-term bank debt, BLOANS(IGOVO,12), and to bring its cash account, CASH(IGOVO), to the level indicated in the flow-of-funds accounts.

7. Pursuant to the Financial Institution Deregulation and Monetary Control Act of March 1980, these interest-rate ceilings are being phased out over the next few years. At that time, the model's ceilings will be set at such high levels they will never be effective.

Chapter 9. Policy Analysis with the Transactions Model

1. Elsewhere we describe experiments with an earlier version of the Transactions Model, in which government programs to hire directly the long-term unemployed or subsidize their employment by private firms were simulated. See Bergmann and Bennett (1977) and Bennett and Bergmann (1980).

Bibliography

Adelman, Irma, and Sherman Robinson, 1978. *Planning for Income Distribution.* Stanford: Stanford University Press.

Almon, Clopper, 1965. *The American Economy to 1975.* New York: Harper & Row.

Arrow, Kenneth, 1951. "Alternative Approaches to the Theory of Choice in Risk Taking Situations." *Econometrica* 19:404–37.

Bennett, Robert L., and Barbara R. Bergmann, 1980. "Policy Explorations with the Transactions Model of the U.S. Economy." In *Microeconomic Simulation Models for Public Policy Analysis,* edited by Robert H. Haveman and Kevin Hollenbeck. New York: Academic Press.

Bergmann, Barbara R., 1974a. "A Microsimulation of the Macroeconomy with Explicitly Represented Money Flows," *Annals of Social and Economic Measurement* 3/3:475–79.

————, 1974b. "Empirical Work on the Labor Market: Is There Any Alternative to Regression Running?" *IRRA Proceedings* 27:243–51.

Bergmann, Barbara R., and Robert L. Bennett, 1977. "Macroeconomic Effects of a Humphrey-Hawkins Type Program," *American Economic Review* 67:265–70.

Blinder, Alan S., 1974. *Toward an Economic Theory of Income Distribution.* Cambridge: MIT Press.

Bosworth, Barry, and James S. Duesenberry, 1974. *A Flow of Funds Model and Its Implications.* Washington, D.C.: Brookings.

Box, George E. P., and Jenkins, Gwilyn M., 1976. *Time Series Analysis: Forecasting and Control.* San Francisco: Holden-Day.

Brechling, Frank, 1965. "The Relationship Between Output and Employment in British Manufacturing Industries," *Review of Economic Studies* 32:187–216.

Coen, Robert M., 1971. "The Effect of Cashflow on the Speed of Adjustment." In *Tax Incentives and Capital Spending,* edited by Gary Fromm. Washington, D.C.: Brookings.

Craine, Roger, Arthur Havenner, and James Berry, 1978. "Fixed Rules vs. Activisim in the Conduct of Monetary Policy," *American Economic Review* 68:769–83.

Cyert, Richard M., and James G. March, 1965. *A Behavioral Theory of the Firm.* Englewood Cliffs, N.J.: Prentice-Hall.

Denison, Edward F., 1962. *The Sources of Economic Growth in the United States and the Alternatives Before Us.* Washington, D.C.: Brookings.

Duesenberry, et al., 1965. *The Brookings Model of the United States Economy.* Chicago: Rand McNally.

Ehrenberg, Ronald G., 1971. "The Impact of the Overtime Premium on Employment and Hours in U.S. Industry," *Western Economic Journal* 9:199–207.

Eichner, Alfred S., 1973. "A Theory of the Determination of the Mark-up Under Oligopoly," *Economic Journal* 83:1184–200.

Eliasson, Gunnar, 1976. *A Micro-Macro Interactive Simulation Model of the Swedish Economy.* Stockholm: Industrial Institute for Economic and Social Research.

Evans, Michael K., 1969. *Macroeconomic Activity: Theory, Forecasting and Control.* New York: Harper & Row.

Fair, Ray C., 1969. *The Short-Run Demand for Workers and Hours.* Amsterdam: North-Holland.

———, 1974. *A Model of Macroeconomic Activity.* New York: Ballinger.

Fischer, Stanley, 1975. "The Demand for Index Bonds," *Journal of Political Economy,* June: 509–34.

———, 1979. "Corporate Supply of Index Bonds," Working Paper 331. Washington, D.C.: National Bureau of Economic Research.

Goldfeld, S. M., and R. E. Quandt, 1972. *Nonlinear Methods in Economics.* Amsterdam: North-Holland.

Gramlich, Edward M., and Dwight M. Jaffee, 1972. *Savings Deposits, Mortgages and Housing.* Lexington, Mass.: Lexington Books.

Grebler, Leo, and Sherman J. Maisel, 1963. "Determinants of Residential Construction: A Review of Present Knowledge." In *Impacts of Monetary Policy,* edited by Commission on Money and Credit. Englewood Cliffs, N.J.: Prentice-Hall.

Hall, R. L., and C. J. Hitch, 1939. "Price Theory and Business Behavior." In *Oxford Studies in the Price Mechanism,* edited by T. Wilson and P. S. Andrews. Oxford: Oxford University Press.

Klein, L. R., and A. S. Goldberger, 1955. *An Econometric Model of the United States, 1929–1952.* Amsterdam: North-Holland.

Kuh, Edwin, 1963. *Capital Stock Growth: A Micro Economic Approach.* Amsterdam: North-Holland.

Lerner, Aaron, 1981. "The Effects of Insider Information on Job Search." Unpublished Ph.D. dissertation, University of Maryland.

Lintner, John, 1956. "Distribution of Incomes of Corporations Among Dividends, Retained Earnings and Taxes," *American Economic Review,* 46: 97–113.

Lutz, Friedrich, and Vera Lutz, 1951. *The Theory of Investment of the Firm.* Princeton: Princeton University Press.

Meyer, John R., and Edwin Kuh, 1957. *The Investment Decision: An Empirical Study.* Cambridge, Mass.: Harvard University Press.

Nelson, Richard R., and Sidney G. Winter, 1982. *An Evolutionary Theory of Economic Change.* Cambridge, Mass.: Harvard University Press.

Nelson, Richard R., Sidney G. Winter, and Herbert L. Schuette, 1976. "Technical Change in an Evolutionary Model," *Quarterly Journal of Economics* 60:90–118.

Nichols, Donald A., 1980. "Is There an Efficient Level of Unemployment? Simulation Experiments on a Labor Market Model." In *Micro Simulation—Models, Methods and Applications,* edited by Barbara Bergmann, Gunnar Eliasson, and Guy Orcutt. Stockholm: Industrial Institute for Economic and Social Research.

Orcutt, Guy, 1960. "Simulation of Economic Systems," *American Economic Review* 50:893–907.

Orcutt, Guy, Steven Caldwell, and Richard Wertheimer II, 1976. *Policy Exploration through Microanalytic Simulation.* Washington, D.C.: Urban Institute.

Parks, Richard W., 1969. "Demand Equations," *Econometrica*, 37:629–650.

Pechman, J. A., and B. A. Okner, 1974. *Who Bears the Tax Burden?* Washington, D.C.: Brookings.

Powell, M. J. D., 1965. "A Method for Minimizing a Sum of Squares of Non-Linear Functions without Calculating Derivatives," *Computer Journal* 7/4:303–7.

Pryor, Frederic L., 1973. "Simulation of the Impact of Social and Economic Institutions on the Size Distribution of Income and Wealth," *American Economic Review* 63:50–72.

Salter, W. E. G., 1960. *Productivity and Technical Change.* Cambridge: Cambridge University Press.

Schultze, Charles L., 1976. "The Economics of the Full Employment and Balanced Growth Act of 1976." Statement before the Senate Committee on Public Welfare, Subcommittee on Unemployment, Poverty, and Migratory Labor, May 14.

Schultze, Charles L., and J. S. Tryon, 1965. "Prices and Wages." In *The Brookings Model of the United States Economy,* edited by Duesenberry et al. Chicago: Rand McNally.

Sheppard, Harold L., and Belitsky, A. Harvey, 1966. *The Job Hunt: Job-Seeking Behavior of Unemployed Workers in a Local Economy.* Baltimore: Johns Hopkins Press.

Solow, R. M., J. Tobin, C. C. Von Weisacker, and M. Yaari, 1966. "Neoclassical Growth with Fixed Factor Proportions," *Review of Economic Studies* 33:79–115.

Weiner, Stuart E., 1983. "Why Are So Few Financial Assets Indexed to Inflation?" *Economic Review,* Federal Reserve Bank of Kansas City, May.

Wonnacott, Paul, 1978. *Macroeconomics.* Homewood, Ill.: Richard D. Irwin.

Index

About the Authors

Robert L. Bennett and Barbara R. Bergmann are both professors of economics at the University of Maryland, where Dr. Bennett also serves as Director of the Computer Laboratory of the Behavioral and Social Sciences Division. He is the author of *The Financial Sector and Economic Development* (Johns Hopkins, 1965) and of articles on development and finance. Dr. Bergmann has written on the subjects of microsimulation methodology, regional growth, input-output analysis, structural unemployment, transportation in development, and employment discrimination and is the author of *The Economic Emergence of American Women* (Basic Books, forthcoming).